Human-Computer Interaction Series

HCI is a multidisciplinary field focused on human aspects of the development of computer technology. As computer-based technology becomes increasingly pervasive—not just in developed countries, but worldwide—the need to take a human-centered approach in the design and development of this technology becomes ever more important. For roughly 30 years now, researchers and practitioners in computational and behavioral sciences have worked to identify theory and practice that influences the direction of these technologies, and this diverse work makes up the field of human-computer interaction. Broadly speaking it includes the study of what technology might be able to do for people and how people might interact with the technology. The HCI series publishes books that advance the science and technology of developing systems which are both effective and satisfying for people in a wide variety of contexts. Titles focus on theoretical perspectives (such as formal approaches drawn from a variety of behavioral sciences), practical approaches (such as the techniques for effectively integrating user needs in system development), and social issues (such as the determinants of utility, usability and acceptability).

For further volumes:
http://www.springer.com/series/6033

María D. Lozano • José A. Gallud
Ricardo Tesoriero • Víctor M.R. Penichet
Editors

Distributed User Interfaces: Usability and Collaboration

 Springer

Editors
María D. Lozano
Computing Systems Department
University of Castilla-La Mancha
Albacete, Spain

José A. Gallud
Computing Systems Department
University of Castilla-La Mancha
Albacete, Spain

Ricardo Tesoriero
Computing Systems Department
University of Castilla-La Mancha
Albacete, Spain

Víctor M.R. Penichet
Computing Systems Department
University of Castilla-La Mancha
Albacete, Spain

ISSN 1571-5035
ISBN 978-1-4471-7245-1   ISBN 978-1-4471-5499-0 (eBook)
DOI 10.1007/978-1-4471-5499-0
Springer London Heidelberg New York Dordrecht

Printed on acid-free paper

Springer is part of Springer Science+Business Media (www.springer.com)

Preface

Distributed User Interfaces (DUIs) have recently become a new field of research and development in Human-Computer Interaction (HCI). DUIs have brought about drastic changes affecting the way interactive systems are conceived. DUIs have gone beyond the fact that user interfaces are controlled by a single end-user on the same computing platform in the same environment.

Traditional interaction is focused on the use of mobile devices such as smartphones, tablets, laptops and so on, tearing apart other environmental interaction resources such as large screens and multi-tactile displays, or tables. Under a collaborative scenario, users sharing common goals may take advantage of DUIs to carry out their tasks because they provide a shared environment where users are allowed to manipulate information in the same space at the same time. Under this hypothesis, collaborative DUI scenarios open new challenges to usability evaluation techniques and methods.

The motivation of this book originated after the 2nd Workshop on Distributed User Interfaces: Collaboration and Usability (DUI 2012), held in Austin, Texas, USA, within the ACM SIGCHI Conference on Human Factors in Computing Systems (CHI 2012). It was then that the editors identified the need for a book which brought together all the interesting contributions that the workshop participants made and the discussion promoted about the emerging topic of DUIs, answering a set of key questions: How can collaboration be improved by using DUIs? In which situations is a DUI suitable to ease the collaboration among users? How can usability standards be employed to evaluate the usability of systems based on DUIs?

The purpose of this book is to present an integrated view of different approaches related to collaboration and usability in distributed user interface settings, which demonstrate the state of the art as well as future directions in this novel and rapidly evolving subject area.

The book is divided into 13 chapters written by relevant researchers in the field of HCI presenting different perspectives and application domains. The contents of these chapters are summarized below:

The first three chapters present foundations and models regarding DUIs. The first chapter entitled "Revisiting the Concept of Distributed User Interfaces" defines key terms to explain the DUI concept and proposes a metamodel able to model any user interface and to classify and characterize it. This work also establishes a conceptual framework of reference for future developments in the field. The second chapter entitled "Improving DUIs with a Decentralized Approach with Transactions and Feedbacks" tackles the problem of multiple users working collaboratively, and the authors propose a decentralized architecture based on a peer-to-peer network providing decentralized transactional support with replicated storage. The third chapter entitled "Distributed UI on Interactive Tabletops: Issues and Context Model" describes an extended context model in order to take into account both interactions on a single interactive tabletop and interactions which are distributed and collaborative.

Chapters 4, 5, 6, 7, and 8 focus on collaboration-related issues. Chapter 4 entitled "Collaborative Content Creation Using Web-Based Distributed User Interface (DUI)" describes collaborative social authoring technology using web-based distributed user interfaces. Chapter 5 entitled "TwisterSearch: A Distributed User Interface for Collaborative Web Search" presents TwisterSearch, a prototype of an interactive and collaborative search system based on DUI. Chapter 6 entitled "Integration of Collaborative Features in Ubiquitous and Context-Aware Systems Using Distributed User Interfaces" presents Ubi4health, a system for healthcare settings that applies the distributed user interface paradigm within ubiquitous environments, which favours the collaborative work. Chapter 7 entitled "A Framework for A Priori Evaluation of Multimodal User Interfaces Supporting Cooperation" describes a new framework for aiding novice designers of highly interactive, cooperative, multimodal systems to make expert decisions in the choice of interaction modalities given the end-users, their activities and the context of use. Finally, Chap. 8 entitled "Enhancing the Security and Usability of DUI Based Collaboration with Proof Based Access Control" addresses the special case of using the anonymous credential system idemix in a project dealing with distributed user interfaces to enhance decision making in disaster situations.

The next two chapters deal with privacy and usability concerns. Chapter 9 entitled "Enhancing LACOME to Consider Privacy and Security Concerns" introduces LACOME, the Large Collaborative Meeting Environment, which is a collaboration system that allows multiple users to simultaneously publish their computer's desktop (workspace) and/or windows on a large shared display via a network connection. In Chap. 10, entitled "Evaluating Usability and Privacy in Collaboration Settings with DUIs: Problem Analysis and Case Studies", the authors present some case studies concerned with evaluating privacy and usability in collaborative settings. The main idea thereby focuses on the involvement of end-users and respective usability and security experts in co-located or distributed settings.

The last three chapters present concrete application domains in which DUIs are applied. Chapter 11 entitled "Distributed and Tangible User Interfaces to Design Interactive Systems for People with Cognitive Disabilities" describes the design of a game-based DUI system aimed at improving cognitive capacities of people with cognitive disabilities. Chapter 12 entitled "Two Thousand Points of Interaction: Augmenting Paper Notes for a Distributed User Experience" presents two early prototypes of a system that couples an augmented wall of paper notes with multiple handheld devices in order to support the process of affinity diagramming. Finally, Chap. 13 entitled "Distributed User Interfaces in a Cloud Educational System" describes the conceptual process developed for the CSchool educational system, which aims to support administration of the educational process by applying distributed user interfaces to cloud services.

We hope that this book will be of interest to a broad audience including academics and researchers interested in collaboration and usability issues on distributed user interface settings.

Finally, we would like to thank all authors for their time and effort in preparing their corresponding chapters. Special thanks to Helen Desmond and Ben Bishop from Springer for all the help provided in editing this volume. We would like also to thank the Editors-in-Chief of the HCI series (John Karat and Jean Vanderdonckt) for giving us the opportunity to prepare this volume.

Albacete, Spain   María D. Lozano

Contents

Contributors

Daniyal M. Alghazzwi IS Department, King Abdulaziz University, Jeddah, Saudi Arabia

Thomas Barth Information Systems Institute – IT Security Group, University of Siegen, Siegen, Germany

Mohamed Bourimi Information Systems Institute – IT Security Group, University of Siegen, Siegen, Germany

Antonio Paules Cipres Albacete Polytechnic School, Information Systems Department, University of Castilla-La Mancha, Albacete, Spain

Gilles Coppin TELECOM Bretagne, Technopôle Brest-Iroise, CS 83818, Brest Cedex 3, France

Sukhveer Dhillon Computer Science, Dalhousie University, Halifax, Canada

Gelek Doksam University of Zurich, Zurich, Switzerland

Habib M. Fardoun Information Systems Department, King Abdulaziz University (KAU), Jeddah, Saudi Arabia

José A. Gallud Computing Systems Department, University of Castilla-La Mancha, Albacete, Spain

Juan E. Garrido Computer Science Research Institute, University of Castilla-La Mancha, Albacete, Spain

Olivier Grisvard TELECOM Bretagne, Technopôle Brest-Iroise, CS 83818, Brest Cedex 3, France

Elena de la Guía Computer Science Research Institute, University of Castilla-La Mancha, Albacete, Spain

Gunnar Harboe University of Zurich, Zurich, Switzerland

Kirstie Hawkey Computer Science, Dalhousie University, Halifax, Canada

Marcel Heupel Information Systems Institute – IT Security Group, University of Siegen, Siegen, Germany

Elaine M. Huang University of Zurich, Zurich, Switzerland

Yves Jaradin Computing Science and Engineering Pole, Université catholique de Louvain, Louvain-la-Neuve, Belgium

Hans-Christian Jetter Intel Collaborative Research Institute for Sustainable Connected Cities (ICRI Cities), University College London, London, UK

Fatih Karatas Information Systems Institute – IT Security Group, University of Siegen, Siegen, Germany

Lukas Keller University of Zurich, Zurich, Switzerland

Dogan Kesdogan Information Systems Institute – IT Security Group, University of Siegen, Siegen, Germany

Christophe Kolski Université Lille Nord de France, Lille, France

UVHC, LAMIH, Valenciennes, France

CNRS, UMR8201, Valenciennes, France

Sébastien Kubicki Lab-STICC UMR6285/UBO/ENIB, European Center for Virtual Reality, Plouzané, France

Yong-Moo Kwon KIST, Seoul, Korea

Magnus Larsson TELECOM Bretagne, Technopôle Brest-Iroise, CS 83818, Brest Cedex 3, France

Changhyeon Lee KIST, Seoul, Korea

Sophie Lepreux Université Lille Nord de France, Lille, France

UVHC, LAMIH, Valenciennes, France

CNRS, UMR8201, Valenciennes, France

María D. Lozano Computing Systems Department, University of Castilla-La Mancha, Albacete, Spain

Boris Mejías Computing Science and Engineering Pole, Université catholique de Louvain, Louvain-la-Neuve, Belgium

Jérémie Melchior Louvain School of Management, Université catholique de Louvain, Louvain-la-Neuve, Belgium

Fathoni Arief Musyaffa KIST, Seoul, Korea

Víctor M. R. Penichet Computing Systems Department, University of Castilla-La Mancha, Albacete, Spain

Franck Poirier Université de Bretagne-Sud, Vannes Cedex, France

Roman Rädle Human-Computer Interaction Group, University of Konstanz, Konstanz, Germany

Harald Reiterer Human-Computer Interaction Group, University of Konstanz, Konstanz, Germany

Peter Van Roy Computing Science and Engineering Pole, Université catholique de Louvain, Louvain-la-Neuve, Belgium

Philipp Schwarte Information Systems Institute – IT Security Group, University of Siegen, Siegen, Germany

Ricardo Tesoriero Computing Systems Department, University of Castilla-La Mancha, Albacete, Spain

Jean Vanderdonckt Louvain School of Management, Université catholique de Louvain, Louvain-la-Neuve, Belgium

Pedro G. Villanueva Computer Science Research Institute, University of Castilla-La Mancha, Albacete, Spain

Chapter 1
Revisiting the Concept of Distributed User Interfaces

Pedro G. Villanueva, Ricardo Tesoriero, and José A. Gallud

Abstract The appearance of a new generation of user interfaces (UI) capable of taking advantage of the diverse and growing ecosystem of interconnected displays has given rise to a new distribution dimension of UIs that are known, up to now, as Distributed User Interfaces (DUI). This new dimension is revolutionizing the way user interfaces are created, designed and used, considering that DUIs give the user the capability to divide the UI and distribute it dynamically among different devices. Through this set of devices, users are capable of completing a task as if it was performed on a traditional UI. Nevertheless, it is necessary to find a formal and precise definition of the concept of DUIs, since the previous ones are either not precise enough, or they do not cover all the existing distribution possibilities. In this work, we define the fundamental terms to explain the DUI concept and we propose a metamodel able to model any user interface and to classify and characterize it as well. This work establishes a conceptual framework of reference for future developments in this field. Finally, five known applications are classified by the proposed metamodel to illustrate the new concepts.

1.1 Introduction

During the last decade the reduction of the price of digital displays has made them very popular among users. Nowadays, users are immersed in ecosystems of displays [1] which are not always related. For instance, a user in a living room may have at his/her disposal a display ecosystem with at least three displays (a smart TV, a laptop screen and a personal smartphone). These devices are not usually related to each other and therefore they run their own applications to achieve different goals.

P.G. Villanueva (✉) • R. Tesoriero • J.A. Gallud
Information System Department, University of Castilla-La Mancha, Campus Universitario de Albacete S/N, 02071 Albacete, Spain
e-mail: pedro.gonzalez@uclm.es; ricardo.tesoriero@uclm.es; jose.gallud@uclm.es

M.D. Lozano et al. (eds.), *Distributed User Interfaces: Usability and Collaboration*,
Human–Computer Interaction Series, DOI 10.1007/978-1-4471-5499-0_1,
© Springer-Verlag London 2013

In a DUI scenario, the user is able to achieve a common goal by using a subset of displays belonging to the same ecosystem. For instance, if the user decides to edit a video in the living room, the video might be displayed on the smart TV, the reproduction may be controlled by the multi-touch screen of the smartphone, and the effects to the video may be applied using the laptop computer. In this scenario, the same user is interacting with many user interfaces at different supported by many platforms pursuing the same goal. It is common to see a user employing in his/her daily work three different computing systems such as a mobile or smartphone, a desktop computer and a tablet. However, the DUI scenario is not limited to single user interaction.

The collaboration scenarios in which various users perform different tasks at the same time have an increasing influence on our everyday lives and have been present for many years. In addition, the applications of these scenarios require that the content is more dynamic and that the users themselves are the content creators. This way, applications allowing the users to share information, interact and do tasks at the same time can be created. One clear example of this type of scenario is the Web 2.0 [2].

Due to the two previously explained tendencies, the proliferation of interactive screens and collaborative scenarios, we are getting more and more demanding with our user interfaces (henceforth referred to as UI) and our need to use the concept of DUI is increasing.

For these reasons, the DUIs are becoming much more prominent every day and it is necessary, therefore, to define the concept of DUI in detail and clearly establish the limits which allow a UI to be differentiated from a DUI. As it will be shown later, there are many definitions for the concept of DUI, but all of them need to be more detailed.

This article revisits the very recent and not well established concept of DUI and introduces new terms related to DUI such as Divisible User Interfaces, Divided States, Distributed States and Unified States. These new terms will be described throughout this article.

The present chapter is organized as follows. This section gives a brief introduction to the work done and its motivation. Section 1.2 shows the state of the art. Subsequently, Sect. 1.3 proposes a new metamodel which includes the characteristics of distribution and allows to classify and characterize the UIs. Section 1.4 presents some case studies which are classified to validate the metamodel. Finally, Sect. 1.5 offers conclusions and future works.

1.2 Related Work

The term Distributed User Interface or DUI has been defined in many different ways and, as it is mentioned in [3], it is not possible to find a single formal definition that can be considered as the reference. The novelty of this paradigm has made that certain applications with some kind of support for distribution are considered as DUI. This section includes some of the most important contributions in this field (for more information about DUI, see also the Chaps. 8, 10, 11 and 13 in this book).

Melchior et al. [4] claim that "a Distributed User Interface consists of a user interface with the capacity to distribute all or part of its components among various monitors, devices, platforms, and/or users."

Authors such as Luyten et al. [5] and Vandervelpen et al. [6] say that "a Distributed User Interface can be divided in parts which migrate to different devices around the final user, and which cooperate to make the user's tasks easier. It is essential to take into account that migration is an essential property of interface distribution".

Berglund and Bang [7] state that "a Distributed User Interface is a user interface which distributes its components among various interactive devices in its environment".

Finally, López et al. [8] conclude that "a Distributed User Interface is the collection of interaction elements that forms a set of User Interfaces, that is to say, a set of elements with a common functionality. These elements are distributed through a set of platforms without losing the common functionality given by the user's task. It is also possible to consider a group of users instead of a single user".

It should also be noted that some authors such as Berti, Paterno, and Santoro [9] refer to DUI as Migratory User Interfaces. The Migratory User Interfaces paradigm is closely related to the concept of DUI in the sense that the user interface as a whole or parts of the user interfaces can be transferred across platforms.

Berti et al. [9] propose a taxonomy which classifies all Migratory User Interfaces according to: activation type (on demand and automatic migration), migration type (total, partial, distributed, incorporating, and multiple), combination of migratory methods (single-method, trans-method, and multiple methods), type of active interfaces (precomputed user interfaces and runtime generation of user interfaces) and so on. In this taxonomy proposal, the authors only take into account the concept of migration, without considering concepts like the division and distribution of the design time and runtime.

As we can conclude from these definitions, there are many different conceptions about what a distributed user interface is, what the consequences of distributing a UI are and how the distribution is implemented. Another consideration is that the definition of DUI is closely related to the concept of UI, which could be considered obvious although the concept of UI is also an evolutionary term with the technology advances [10].

Among all the reviewed literature, the studies of Melchior [4], Vandervelpen [6] and López [8] stand out because all of them present the concept of DUI and its most important properties.

The only formal definition of the concept of DUI can be found in the research of López [8], for whom the only DUI is the collection of UIs that are run on a collection of platforms and which have the common goal of carrying out the user's tasks. This definition represents a step forward in the formalization of the concept of DUI.

All these previous definitions and conceptions about what the inclusion of the distribution dimension in the user interface means are not complete enough since they do not cover all the possible distribution configurations, which can be proved because they fail to answer the following questions:

1. How can we distinguish the case of a UI that can be divided and distributed in runtime from an application that has a UI which was previously divided and distributed in design time? Should we consider design time versus runtime DUIs division and distribution relevant?
2. If we run an application UI on a PC that supports multiple monitors, can we consider this application UI a DUI?
3. Is a divisible UI a DUI? Is a divided UI a DUI?
4. How many different types of DUIs exist?

It can be demonstrated that it is not possible to respond to these questions with the presented definitions, and therefore previous definitions of DUIs cannot be used to cover the wide spectrum of configurations that gives way to the division and distribution of UIs. The redefinition of the concept of DUI, which is formally presented in this article, provides a new perspective to understand the implications of dividing and distributing UIs.

1.3 Distributed User Interfaces Characterization

The metamodel shown in Fig. 1.1 presents the distribution characteristics. Any user interface (UI) can be modeled with the metamodel. MOF enriched with OCL constraints has been used to establish the formal definition of the metamodel.

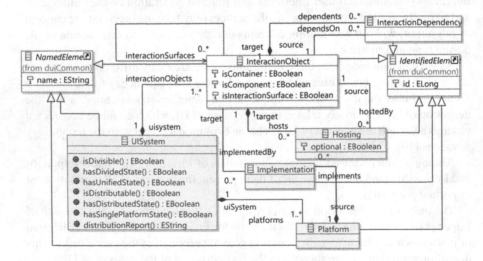

Fig. 1.1 Distribution conceptual metamodel for user interfaces

This section describes the concepts presented in Fig. 1.1 and the invariants that establish certain restrictions that the metamodel cannot represent by itself. Besides, a classification based on the concepts presented is proposed.

1.3.1 Concepts

The concepts presented in Fig. 1.1 can be described as following:

UISystem: The UISystem entity is the central element of the proposed metamodel and it represents the user interface of an interactive application. Some examples are: the Calculator application, the Paint.NET,[1] the GIMP,[2] the Marca[3] web application, the EcoPanels [11].

Platform: The Platform entity is the combination of Hardware (CPU and I/O devices) and the operating system which supports the running application. In the case of Web applications, the browser is part of the platform. Therefore, instances of Platform metaclass define the "variable of platform" concept as the representation of a platform in a distribution environment.

InteractionObject: The InteractionObject entity (hereafter referred to as IO) is defined as the Abstract Interaction Object (AIO) described in [12].

Hosting: The Hosting entity establishes a relationship between two IO. If an IO has several alternatives to be hosted, it means that this IO may be in some of the hosts or in all of them, but at least in one.

Implementation: The Implementation entity represents an IO which is supported or can be run on a Platform.

InteractionComponent: The InteractionComponent entity represents the basic elements of the user interface. An InteractionComponent cannot contain other elements. An IO is an InteractionComponent when the isComponent calculated property has value of "true". IsComponent property is calculated in OCL as follows:

```
Context InteractionObject:: isComponent: Boolean
derive: hosts->isEmpty()
```

Some examples are: a button, a label, an icon of a RFID panel, etc.

InteractionContainer: The InteractionContainer entity represents user interface elements able to contain other elements. An IO is an InteractionContainer when the isContainer calculated property has a value of "true". IsContainer property is calculated in OCL as following:

```
ContextInteractionObject:: isContainer: Boolean
derive: not hosts->isEmpty()
```

---

[1]http://www.getpaint.net
[2]http://www.gimp.org
[3]http://www.marca.com

Some examples are: a grid including two buttons, a region of a RFID panel that contains some RFID icons, etc.

InteractionSurface: The InteractionSurface entity represents user interface elements that may contain other elements, but that cannot be contained in another element. An IO is an InteractionSurface when the isInteractionSurface calculated property has a value of "true". IsInteractionSurface property is calculated in OCL as following:

```
Context InteractionObject:: isInteractionSurface:
  Boolean
derive: not hosts->isEmpty() and not implementedBy->
  isEmpty()
```

Some examples are: a windows desktop, a panel of RFID, an Activity on Android, a Page on Windows Phone, a View on iPhone, etc.

InteractionDependency: The InteractionDependency entity represents an IO which depends on another IO. This relationship can only occur between two ISs, and if an IS disappears, all the ISs that depend on it disappear.

We can see an example of InteractionDependency in the Paint.NET application. There is an IS_1 which corresponds to the Paint.NET main window and another IS_2 that corresponds to the tool window. We can consider that IS_2 depends on IS_1 because if we close IS_1, IS_2 alsocloses, but not vice versa.

Since the Hosting relationship establishes the possibility that an IO is hosted or not in another, models generated with the metamodel can be interpretedas states models. Each states model has all the possible states that an application can reach.

State: A state is the organization of all the IOs of the UISystem and the Platforms that implements the IOs at a given moment.

The IO entity has two calculated properties to facilitate the analysis of the generated models. These properties are platforms and interactionSurfaces. The **platforms** property provides the set of Platforms on which IO can run. The expression in OCL that calculates this property is:

```
Context InteractionObject:: platforms: Set(Platform)
derive: self.interactionSurfaces.implementedBy->
flatten().oclAsType(Implementation).source->
  asSet()->asSet()
->union(self.implementedBy.source->asSet())->
  asOrderedSet()
```

The **interactionSurfaces** property provides the set of ISs on which the IO can be hosted. The expression in OCL that calculates this property is:

```
Context InteractionObject:: interactionSurfaces:
  Set(InteractionSurface)
derive: self->closure(hostedBy.target)->
select(isInteractionSurface)
```

1.3.2 Invariants

It is necessary to define a set of invariants to establish certain restrictions because these restrictions must be maintained and cannot be expressed directly in the proposed metamodel.

ComponentCannotBeInteractionSurface: An InteractionComponent cannot be an IS. This invariant is required because the model does not control that an IO can be an InteractionComponent and an IS at the same time. The OCL expression for this invariant is:

```
Context InteractionObject
inv componentCannotBeInteractionSurface: isComponent
    implies not isInteractionSurface
```

Cycle: Models created with the proposed metamodel are graphs. These graphs should not contain cycles because an IO cannot host any of their ancestors. The OCL expression for this invariant is:

```
Context InteractionObject
inv cycle: not self->closure(hostedBy.target)->
    includes(self)
```

DependenciesOnInteractionSurfaces: This invariant restricts that only an InteractionDependency relationship can be established between two ISs. The OCL expression for this invariant is:

```
Context InteractionObject
inv cycle: not self->closure(hostedBy.target)->
    includes(self)
```

HostingTheSameInteractionObjectTwice: This invariant restricts that an IO cannot be more than once in the same IO. The OCL expression for this invariant is:

```
Context InteractionObject
inv hostingTheSameInteractionObjectTwice:
source.hostedBy->forAll(h : Hosting | h <> self implies
    h.target<>self.target)
```

1.3.3 User Interfaces Classification

The UISystem entity has a set of operations; these operations allow us to characterize the modelled user interface. Some operations can classify the UISystem and other operations can detect possible states that can be achieved. This section presents the proposed classification and the most representative states.

Classification

An application or UISystem can be considered in our distribution classification as Divisible/Undivisible, Distributable/Undistributable. Let us explain the meaning of these attributes:

Divisible UISystem

A UISystem is divisible, if and only if, there is at least one IO that can be hosted in more than one IS. This property is calculated by isDivisible operation. The OCL expression for this operation is as follows:

```
ContextUISystem:: isDivisible(): Boolean
body: self.interactionObjects->exists(io :
  InteractionObject | io->interactionSurfaces->
  size() > 1)
```

Distributable UISystem

A UISystem is distributable, if and only if, there is at least one IO which can be in more than one platform. This property is calculated by the isDistributable operation. The OCL expression for this operation is as follows:

```
ContextUISystem:: isDistributable(): Boolean
body: self.interactionObjects->exists(io :
  InteractionObject | io.platforms->size() > 1)
```

States

As it has already been mentioned, the models obtained from the proposed meta-model can be seen as states models. Therefore, an application or UISystem in a specific moment of its execution is located in some of these states. We should be able to calculate from a states model whether the UISystem can reach a specific type of state. The most representative states are described in the next paragraphs.

Unified State: A UISystem has a unified state, if and only if, among all ISs at least there is one that does not depend on any other IS. This state is calculated by the hasUnifiedState operation. The OCL expression for this operation is as follows:

```
ContextUISystem:: hasUnifiedState(): Boolean
body: not self.interactionObjects->select
  ((isInteractionSurface and dependsOn->isEmpty()))->
  isEmpty()
```

Divided State: A UISystem has a divided state, if and only if, it has more than one IS. This state is calculated by the hasDividedState operation. The OCL expression for this operation is as follows:

```
ContextUISystem:: hasDividedState(): Boolean
body: self.interactionObjects->select
  (isInteractionSurface)-> size() > 1
```

Distributed State: A UISystem has a distributed state, if and only if, it has at least two ISs implemented on different Platforms. This state is calculated by the hasDistributedState operation. The OCL expression for this operation is as follows:

```
ContextUISystem:: hasDistrubutedState(): Boolean
body: self.interactionObjects->exists(io1 :
  InteractionObject, io2 : InteractionObject |
  io1 <> io2 and
notio1.platforms->symmetricDifference(io2.platforms)
  ->isEmpty())
```

A Single Platform State: A UISystem has a single platform state, if and only if, all IOs can be contained in a single platform. This state is calculated by the hasASinglePlatformState operation. The OCL expression for this operation is as follows:

```
ContextUISystem:: hasSinglePlatformState(): Boolean
body: not self.interactionObjects->iterate(io :
  InteractionObject; res : Set(Platform) =
  self.platforms |
res->intersection(io.platforms))->isEmpty()
```

1.4   Case Studies

In this section we put into practice the proposed metamodel. In this way, five applications among the most representative ones are modeled in this section to illustrate the classification and discuss the possible states. For each case study, the model is generated, is validated against the metamodel, and then, a set of properties is obtained with the operations presented in Sect. 1.3.3.

Because the complete case study models are very extensive, we decided to present a simplified version of them. The five case studies have been modeled with the editor that was developed as plugin[4] for Eclipse and is based in the metamodel. You can see how to design models with the model editor in the video.[5]

1.4.1   Classifying Case Studies

The first case study is the Paint.NET application. The Paint.NET is a tool for editing images. Figure 1.2a shows the application interface and the Fig. 1.2b displays the model corresponding to the application.

---

[4]Editor for Eclipse: http://dui.uclm.es/taxonomy/site
[5]Demo of DUI Editor: http://www.youtube.com/watch?v=lTjgqIPVS_Y

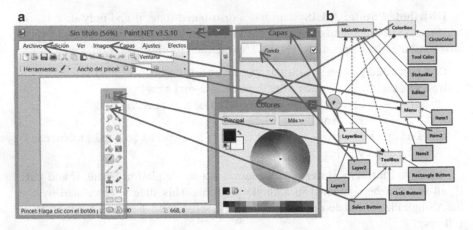

Fig. 1.2 Paint.NET case study. (**a**) User interface, (**b**) simplified distributed model

According to the metamodel, this application has a non-divisible and non-distributable UISystem. In addition, it can achieve at least one unified state, at least one divided state, at least one of single platform state and it cannot reach a distributed state.

The UISystem is not divisible because there are no IO that can be in two different ISs. It is not distributable because there is only a platform. The UISystem has a unified state because the ToolBox, ColorBox and LayerBox ISs can disappear and become only the MainWindow IS. It has a divided state because it has four ISs and a single platform state because it only has a platform. A distributed state cannot be achieved because it can only be on one platform.

The second case study is the GIMP 2.7 application. This application is a tool for editing images. Figure 1.3a shows the application interface and the Fig. 1.3b displays the model corresponding to the application.

According to the metamodel, this application has a divisible and non-distributable UISystem. In addition, it cannot reach a unified state, can reach at least one divided state, at least one single platform state and it cannot reach a distributed state.

The UISystem is divisible because for example the ToolSettings can be a IS or be contained in the ToolBox IS. It is not distributable because there is only a platform. The UISystem does not have a unified state because all IS depend on some. It has a divided state because it has four ISs and a single platform state because it only has a platform. And a distributed State cannot be reach because it can only be on one platform.

The third case study is WallShare. WallShare is a system to share resources in face-to-face meetings, as it is explained in detail in the work [13]. Figure 1.4a shows the application interface and the Fig. 1.4a displays the model corresponding to the application. According to the metamodel, this application has a not divisible and not distributable UISystem. In addition, it can reach a unified state, can reach at least

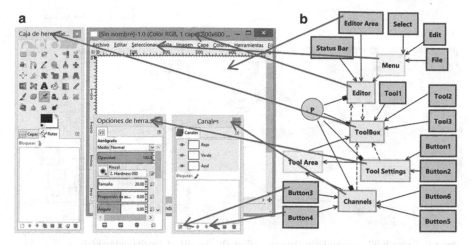

Fig. 1.3 GIMP case study. (**a**) User interface, (**b**) simplified distributed model

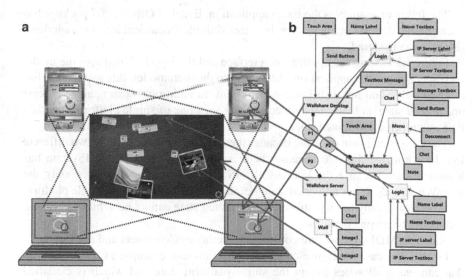

Fig. 1.4 WallShare case study. (**a**) User interface, (**b**) simplified distributed model

one divided state, cannot reach a single platform state and can reach at least one distributed state.

The UISystem is not divisible because there are no IO that can be in two different ISs. It is not distributable because there is only a platform. The UISystem has a unified state because no IS depends on the rest. It has a divided state because it has three ISs. It does not have a single platform state because the three ISs cannot be on the same platform. And it has at least one distributed state because each IO is in a different platform.

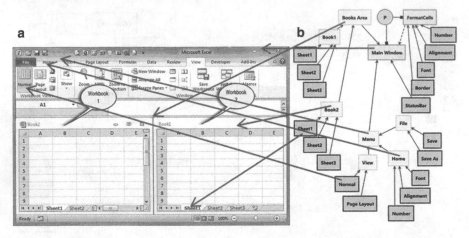

Fig. 1.5 Excel 2007 case study. (**a**) User interface, (**b**) simplified distributed model

The fourth case study is the Excel application. Excel of Office 2007 package has been chosen as a case study to show how the Multiple Document Interface windows (MDI) are considered.

Figure 1.5a shows the application interface and the Fig. 1.5b displays the model corresponding to the application. According to the metamodel, this application has a not divisible and not distributable UISystem. In addition, it can achieve at least one unified state, at least one divided state, at least one of single platform state and it cannot reach a distributed state.

The UISystem is not divisible because there are no IO that can be in two different ISs. It is not distributable because there is only a platform. The UISystem has a unified state because the FormatCells IS can disappear and become only the MainWindow IS. It has a divided state because it has two ISs and a single platform state because it only has a platform. A distributed state cannot be achieved because it can only be on one platform.

Note that MDI windows are considered InteractionContainers and not ISs.

Finally, the case study presented in [14] is a clear example of an application that can reach all states except the single platform state and which is classified as divisible and distributable. Figure 1.6a shows the application interface and the Fig. 1.6b displays the model corresponding to the application. According to the metamodel, this application has a divisible and distributable UISystem. In addition, it can reach all states discussed in Sect. 1.3.3 except the single platform state.

The UISystem is divisible and distributable because the Quiz, GroupImages and ChooseResponse IOs can go each one of them to different ISs on different platforms. The UISystem has at least one unified state because no IS depends on the rest. It has at least one divided state because it has four ISs. It cannot reach a single platform state because the four ISs cannot be on the same platform. And it has at least one distributed state because each IO is in a different platform.

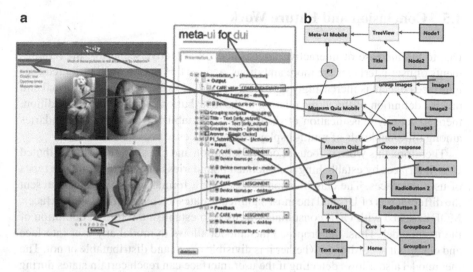

Fig. 1.6 Quiz case study. (**a**) User interface, (**b**) simplified distributed model

Table 1.1 Classification and characterization of cases studies

	Classification		States			
Case studies	Divisible	Distributable	Unified state	Divided state	A single platform state	Distributed state
Paint.NET	✘	✘	✔	✔	✔	✘
GIMP 2.7	✔	✘	✘	✔	✔	✘
WallShare	✘	✘	✔	✔	✘	✔
Excel 2007	✘	✘	✔	✔	✔	✘
Quiz	✔	✔	✔	✔	✘	✔

1.4.2 Summary of Results

The five case studies were classified and characterized and the results are shown in Table 1.1. A first classification group takes into account the "Divisible" and "Distributable" features. The second group shows the different states.

Following our definitions and the proposed metamodel, the Quiz prototype can be classified as "Divisible" and "Distributable" while the GIMP is classified as "Divisible". These two applications have more distribution capabilities than the rest of the analyzed applications. In general, an application with the ability to move an Interaction Object among two different window frames or similar (Interaction Surfaces), could be classified as "Divisible", while an application to move an Interaction Object among platforms could be classified as "Distributable".

1.5 Conclusion and Future Work

Due to the increase of interactive screens and collaborative scenarios, the requirements of user interfaces are more ambitious, and for this reason the distributed user interface concept is increasingly more widespread. However, there is no formal and precise definition of the terms relating to the distribution of interfaces. In addition, there is not any classification of distribution to establish well-defined boundaries among different kinds of multi-display user interfaces.

Therefore, this work is focused on the definition and classification of Distributed User Interfaces by establishing well-defined boundaries between the different types of user interfaces. The classification is based on a formal metamodel to represent the different sets of UIs and the most significant states to characterize the interfaces. MOF enriched with OCL constraints was used to establish the formal definition of the metamodel. Thus, the proposed metamodel allows to model any user interface and classify it according to whether it is divisible or not and distributable or not. The metamodel also allows detecting if the user interface can reach certain states during its execution. These states are: unified, divided, single platform and distributed.

The formal definition proposed in this chapter allows us to respond to the questions raised in Sect. 1.2. The answers are as follows:

1. Considering the new proposal, there is no difference between design and runtime to classify a particular UI from the division and distribution perspective. In design time we can know if an application is Divisible or Distributable and the possible states that it can achieve. In runtime, we can only know the application's state in a given time.
2. If an application only supports a platform, the application cannot be a DUI. If the application has an InteractionSurface (IS) in each monitor, we can only affirm that the application is in a divided state.
3. According to the definitions, we can say that a Divisible UISystem does not imply to be Distributable (See Sect. 1.3.3.1). Accordingly, "divided" is a UI state and has nothing to do with distribution.
4. There is only one kind of DUI, but a UI can reach certain states or not, as for instance, unified or divided (See Sect. 1.3.3.2).

As future work we will advance in the metamodel to incorporate distribution primitive (copy, clone, distribute, show, hide, etc.) on the InteractionObjects.

In addition, the new definitions can introduce different levels of division or distribution, defining a degree of division of distribution. In this way, we will be able to study how the division or distribution degrees affect the users' task.

Acknowledgments We thank the CICYT-TIN 2011-27767-C02-01 Spanish project from the Ministerio de Economía y Competitividad, the PPII10-0300-4174 and the PII2C09-0185-1030 JCCM Projects for supporting this research. We also would like to thank to the "Programa de Potenciación de Recursos Humanos" from the Scientific Research, Technological Development and Innovation Regional Plan 2011–2015(PRINCET).

References

1. Terrenghi, T., Quigley, A., & Dix, A. (2009). A taxonomy for and analysis of multi-person-display ecosystems. *Personal and Ubiquitous Computing, 13*(8), 583–598.
2. O'Reilly, T. (2005). What is web 2.0? Design patterns and business models for the next generation of software. http://www.oreillynet.com/lpt/a/6228
3. Elmqvist, N. (2011). Distributed user interfaces: State of the art. In *Proceedings of the 1st workshop on distributed user interfaces in conjunction with CHI 2011* (pp. 7–12). University of Castilla-La Mancha. ISBN 978-84-693-9829-6. Vancouver, 7 May 2011.
4. Melchior, J., Grolaux, D., Vanderdonckt, J., & Van, R. P. (2009). A toolkit for peer-to-peer distributed user interfaces: Concepts, implementation, and applications. *Proceedings of the 1st ACM SIGCHI Symposium on Engineering Interactive Computing Systems* (pp. 69–78), Pittsburgh.
5. Luyten, K., & Coninx, K. (2005). Distributed user interface elements to support smart interaction spaces. *Proceeding of the 7th IEEE International Symposium on Multimedia, IEEE Computer Society* (pp. 277–286), Washington, DC.
6. Vandervelpen, Ch., Vanderhulst, K., Luyten, K., & Coninx, K. (2005). Light-weight distributed web interfaces: Preparing the web for heterogeneous environments. *Proceeding of 5th International Conference on Web Engineering. ICWE'2005*. Berlin: Springer-Verlag.
7. Berglund, E., & Bang, M. (2002). Requirements for distributed user-interfaces in ubiquitous computing networks. *Proceedings of MUM2002*. Oulu, 11–13 Dec 2002.
8. López, J. J., Gallud, J. A., Lazcorreta, E., Peñalver, A., & Botella, F. (2011). Distributed user interfaces: Specification of essential properties. In *Distributed user interfaces: Designing interfaces for the distributed ecosystem* (pp. 13–21). New York: Springer. Chapter 2. ISBN 978-1-4471-2270-8.
9. Berti, S., Paternó, F., & Santoro, C. (2006). A taxonomy for migratory user interfaces. In S. W. Gilroy & M. D. Harrison (Eds.), *DSV-IS 2005* (LNCS, Vol. 3941, pp. 149–160). Heidelberg: Springer.
10. Calvary, G., Coutaz, J., Thevenin, D., Limbourg, Q., Bouillon, L., & Vanderdonckt, J. (2003). A unifying reference framework for multi-target user interfaces. *Interacting with Computers, 15*(3), 289–308.
11. Tesoriero, R., Tébar, R., Gallud, J. A., Penichet, V. M. R., & Lozano, M. (2008). Interactive ecopanels: Paneles ecológicos interactivos basados en RFID. *Proceedings of the IX Congreso Internacional de Interacción Persona-Ordenador Interacción* 2008 (pp. 155–165). ISBN:978-84-691-3871-7.
12. Vanderdonckt, J., & Bodart, F. (1993). Encapsulating knowledge for intelligent automatic interaction objects selection. In S. Ashlund et al. (Eds.), *Proceedings of InterCHI'93 "Bridges Between Worlds"* (Amsterdam, 24–29 Apr 1993) (pp. 424–429). New York: ACM Press.
13. Villanueva, P. G., Tesoriero, R., & Gallud, J. A. (2010). Multipointer and collaborative system for mobile devices. *Proceedings of the 12th International Conference on Human Computer Interaction with Mobile Devices and Services* (pp. 435–438), ACM Press.
14. Manca, M., & Paternò, F. (2011). Distributing user interfaces with MARIA. *Distributed User Interfaces 2011 (DUI 2011), CHI 2011 Workshop* (pp. 93–96). Vancouver, 7–12 May 2011.

Chapter 2
Improving DUIs with a Decentralized Approach with Transactions and Feedbacks

Jérémie Melchior, Boris Mejías, Yves Jaradin, Peter Van Roy, and Jean Vanderdonckt

Abstract When multiple users work collaboratively, coherence is not an easy feature to guarantee. It requires an exclusive access to some part of the User Interface (UI) and needs to give some feedbacks to other users. This synchronization needs a true concurrency control algorithm. One of the most common solution is to use a server as a transactional manager. Unfortunately, a central point of control is also a single point of failure. This paper proposes a decentralized architecture based on a peer-to-peer network providing decentralized transactional support with replicated storage. As a consequence, there is a gain in fault-tolerance and the transactional protocol eliminates the problem of network delay improving the overall usability. The addition of a feedback mechanism allow the users to understand better the behavior of the system.

2.1 Introduction

There are many software applications supporting collaborative work, such as drawing, text editing or software development. Collaborative work can be done synchronously or asynchronously. In the latter case, the participants make their modifications on their local copy without direct interaction with the other participants. Once the changes are made, they are committed to the global state. In the former case, which is the focus of this paper, all participants are concurrently working on a shared working space. Such scenario requires continuous synchronization of the

J. Melchior (✉) • J. Vanderdonckt
Louvain School of Management, Université catholique de Louvain, Louvain-la-Neuve, Belgium
e-mail: Jeremie.Melchior@uclouvain.be; Jean.Vanderdonckt@uclouvain.be

B. Mejías • Y. Jaradin • P. Van Roy
Computing Science and Engineering Pole, Université catholique de Louvain,
Louvain-la-Neuve, Belgium
e-mail: Boris.Mejias@uclouvain.be; Yves.Jaradin@uclouvain.be; Peter.VanRoy@uclouvain.be

M.D. Lozano et al. (eds.), *Distributed User Interfaces: Usability and Collaboration*,
Human–Computer Interaction Series, DOI 10.1007/978-1-4471-5499-0_2,
© Springer-Verlag London 2013

participants in order to avoid conflicts. One way of achieving such synchronization is by letting the participants lock the part of the shared space they want to modify, granting exclusive access to that part. Since all participants can take any lock, having a single point of control make sense, resulting in the classical client–server architecture. Unfortunately, it is well known that having a single point of control also means having a single point of failure, because the whole application relies on the stability of the server.

The case study we present in the paper is based on TransDraw [1]; a distributed collaborative vector-based graphical editor with a shared drawing area. Each user runs the application and joins a server to get access to the shared area. When someone is drawing in this area, feedback is sent to other users reflecting the action. In addition, TransDraw uses a transactional protocol to allow users to make optimistic changes on the drawing with immediate conflict resolution. This feature eliminates the problem of performance degradation caused by network latency and it is a crucial property of TransDraw. The synchronization and storage of the global state is done on a server which centralizes the control of the work flow. When users modify an object on the drawing, they request exclusive access for it, which may succeed or fail depending on the behavior of the other users. All this is reflected graphically in the shared drawing space.

A problem of TransDraw, due to its centralized architecture, is its dependency on the server. If the server crashes the work is lost, and the application will not run until the server is rebooted. Peer-to-peer networks have the nice property of being self-organized, fault-tolerant and fully decentralized. We propose in this paper to redesign the transactional protocol of TransDraw to overcome the problem of the single point of failure. In order to do that, we use Beernet, a structured peer-to-peer overlay network providing a fault-tolerant distributed transaction layer with replicated storage. Every time a user attempts to modify a graphical object, this modification will be done inside a transaction with a different transaction manager, which is replicated to allow the transaction to finish in case of failure of the manager. Unfortunately, this fault-tolerance mechanism is not free. Replication requires a higher usage of network resources increasing latency of transactions, but the optimistic approach for starting the modification of an object counteracts the latency. We consider this a small drawback because the functionality of TransDraw is fully respected and there is an important gain in fault-tolerance.

For the management of DUIs another problem comes from the needs of feedback. The initiator of the distribution must know when the distribution is over and if everything went well. The destination platform should notice the distribution and not be affected negatively by it. For this, we use a feedback mechanism in order to notify both the source and the destination for any kind of distribution. If the result of the distribution is invisible to one of them, a feedback needs to ensuré the action went well. If the result is creating information or modifying the destination remotely, the destination should understand this addition or change

What follows is a more detailed description of TransDraw and related works in Sects. 2.2 and 2.3. Beernet is described in Sect. 2.4. The core of the proposal is explained in Sect. 2.5, being followed by the conclusions.

2.2 Transdraw

2.2.1 Description

Transdraw is a collaborative vector drawing tool created by Donatien Grolaux using transactions [2]. The toolbar provides, not only the traditional tools of vector editing (e.g. lines, ellipse, rectangles), but also a pair of tools supporting collaboration. As soon as a user selects an object, a request is sent to the server for the corresponding lock. However, the user is permitted to edit the object optimistically before the server can answer the request. The optimistic nature of the operation is visually presented to the user by feedback in the form of a red selection frame. When the server grants the lock, the transaction on the object is committed and the user can continue to edit the object in exclusive mode, indicated by black selection handles until he deselects it at which time the lock will be returned. If the lock was already held by another user, the server has to refuse it to the user and the transaction is aborted. The user sees the modifications he did optimistically undo themselves and the object is deselected.

A user can also manage explicitly his locks by using the *take lock* tool, for example to make a complex reorganization of the drawing, involving several individual objects. He then has to release the locks manually using the flashing *release-locks* button. In order to prevent starvation which could happen as simply as by a user inadvertently selecting every object before taking a rest, a lock stealing mechanism is provided. The *steal lock* tool make a request to steal a lock to the server which forwards it to the current owner of the lock. This user then has a few seconds to accept or reject the stealing of her locks. On timeout, the stealing is considered accepted. Once accepted, the previous owner notifies the server to forward the lock to the stealer.

2.2.2 Example Scenario

Figure 2.1 presents the view of two users working on the same drawing, each in his own window. Bob, on the right, had the top ellipse selected long enough for the server to grant him the lock as can be seen by the black selection handles around it. Alice, on the left has just tried to select this ellipse. After a, normally brief, period during which she was able to do optimistic changes to this ellipse, her transaction is aborted, and she is notified of it by the disappearance of her selection and the red dot on the ellipse which will blink a few times to explain that Bob is a currently editing this object.

The diagram in Fig. 2.2 describes a possible continuation of the scenario in which Alice steals the lock from Bob to perform the update she wants. Alice ask to steal the lock to the server. Since Bob currently has the lock, the server ask Bob whether he

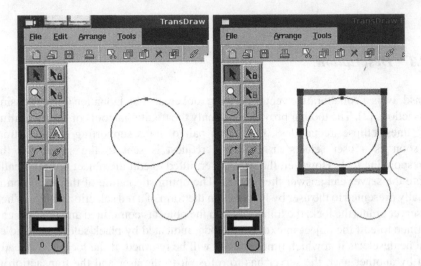

Fig. 2.1 Alice, on the *left*, see a locked and non-editable ellipse while Bob has it is selected and editable

Fig. 2.2 Scenario of complex interaction

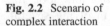
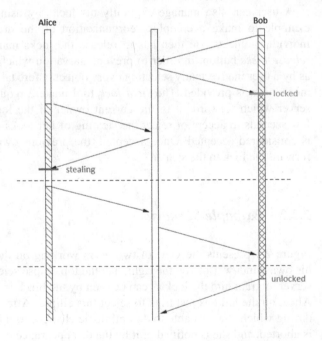

allows his lock to be stolen or not. This is shown to Bob as two blinking buttons at the bottom of his edition window as we can see in Fig. 2.3. If Bob allows his lock to be stolen, either explicitly or by ignoring the request long enough, he loose selection of the object and possession of the lock and the server transfer them to Alice.

All of this assumes that the server does not crash.

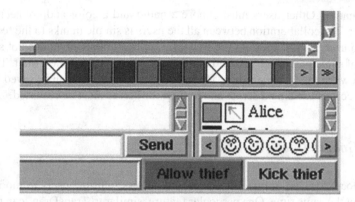

Fig. 2.3 Bob is asked whether he allows his lock to be stolen

2.3 Related Works

There are some applications that already support collaboration in different ways.
We describe and comment some of them briefly.

2.3.1 BOUML

BOUML [3] is a free UML tool that allows drawing diagrams and generating code
in multiple languages. The tool has been developed as a multiuser application in a
sequential way. Each user of the application must choose an identifier which allows
working on some diagrams. The work may be done in parallel but there is not any
feedback on other users' work as there is no support for concurrent work. There
are many problems with the tool. The lack of feedback prevents user to know what
others are doing and to see their changes. It is also impossible to know which files
are currently being modified or that have been modified and saved. There can be
conflicts when saving the project. When users are working collaboratively, the work
of a user will be saved but not all the modification of other users. This leads to
irreversible lost work without any warning. Another problem is the impossibility to
lock part of the work to prevent modification from another user.

2.3.2 Gobby

Gobby is a free text-editor that allows collaborative work [4]. It supports multiuser
parallel edition on multiple documents and a multiuser chat. A user has to start
a session and create the documents, he will host the server needed to centralize

the information. Other users must choose a name and a color and connect to the server host. The collaboration between all the users is simple thanks to the feedback brought to users with colors. As the BOUML application, Gobby does not support any lock of some part of the text and all the users can edit what they want. There is a problem when the server crashes. The unsaved modifications can be saved but the whole process of creating a server and joining the server must be restarted.

2.3.3 Google Docs

Google Docs [5] is an online office suite that allows multiple users to modify the same file at the same time. One particular feature, similar to TransDraw, can be seen on spreadsheets. Once a user is modifying a cell, this one is colored differently as in any single user spreadsheet application. When other users connect to Google servers to edit the same file, then, the cells they select will appear with a different color on the view of the other users, and with a tag identifying the user. Instead of locking the cell, changes are save incrementally using versioning. Google Docs uses also a centralized architecture because everything is controlled at Google side. But, there is a very important difference. There is not only one server to rely on, but a set of servers with replicated information, so if a server crashes, another one takes over. Of course, these are only conjectures about Google's back-end.

2.4 Decentralized Transactional DHT

Beernet [6] is a structured overlay network providing a distributed hash table (DHT) with symmetric replication. Peers are self-organized using the relaxed-ring topology [7], which is derived from Chord [8], with cost-efficient ring maintenance and self-healing properties. Data replication is guaranteed with a decentralized transactional protocol allowing the modification of different items within a single transaction. The transactional protocol implements a Paxos-consensus algorithm [2, 9], which requires the agreement of the majority of peers holding the replicas of the items. We will focus on the transactional layer of Beernet because it will be our mean to decentralize TransDraw.

Figure 2.4 describes how the Paxos-consensus protocol works. The client, which is connected to a peer that is part of the network, triggers a transaction in order to read/write some items from the global store. When the transaction begins, the peer becomes the transaction manager (TM) for that particular transaction. The whole transaction is divided in two phases: *read phase* and *commit phase*. During the *read phase*, the TM contact all transaction participants (TPs) for all the items involved in the transaction. TPs are chosen from the peers holding a replica of the items. The modification to the data is done optimistically without requesting any lock yet. Once all the read/write operations are done, and the client decides to commit the transaction, the *commit phase* is started.

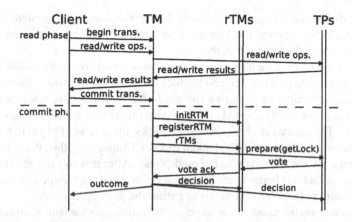

Fig. 2.4 Paxos consensus protocol for distributed transactions

In order to commit the changes on the replicas, it is necessary to get the lock of the majority of TPs for all items. But, before requesting the locks, it is necessary to register a set of replicated transaction managers (rTMs) that are able to carry on the transaction in case that the TM crashes. The idea is to avoid locking TPs forever. Once the rTMs are registered, the TM sends a *prepare* message to all participants. This is equivalent to request the lock of the item. The TPs answer back with a $vote$ to all TMs (arrow to TM removed for legibility). The vote is acknowledged by all rTMs to the leader TM. Like that, the TM will be able to take a decision if the majority of rTMs have enough information to take exactly the same decision. If the TM crashes at this point, another rTM can take over the transaction. The decision will be *commit* if the majority of TPs voted for commit. It will be *abort* otherwise. Once the decision is received by the TPs, locks are released.

The protocol provides atomic commit on all replicas with fault tolerance on the transaction manager and the participants. As long as the majority of TMs and TPs survives the process, the transaction will correctly finish. These are very strong properties that will allows us to run TransDraw on a decentralized system without depending on a server.

2.5 Decentralized TransDraw

Instead of using a big infrastructure, we can achieve replication and fault-tolerance by building TransDraw on top of a peer-to-peer network, and by decentralizing the synchronization of locks and data storage. Our proposal is to build TransDraw on top of Beernet.

The Paxos-consensus protocol as described in Sect. 2.4 is not sufficient to provide exactly the same functionality of TransDraw as it was described in Sect. 2.2.

The main difference lies on the moment where the locks are granted. As it is currently, locks are granted too late for TransDraw, because it is not possible to inform users about the intention of the others.

The first modification we have to do to the transactional protocol is to allow eager locking request. One idea is to request the locks when read/write operations are sent to the transaction participants during the *read-phase*. If locks are not granted, the transaction is immediately aborted. The problem introduced by this modification is that if leader TM crashes after requesting the locks, there is no rTM yet to take over the transaction, and items would be locked forever. Considering this, the registration of rTMs must also be moved up to the read-phase. After this two modifications we realized that in fact it is better to avoid the read-phase and start immediately with an extended commit phase that first needs to gather the participants.

The second modification is an eager notification mechanism. Currently, out transactional layer is meant for asynchronous access to the share state. When a peer writes a new value for item, other users are not notified unless they read the item. In the case of TransDraw, other users not only need to be notified of every modification on the value of items, but also on the intention of other users when they lock items. To achieve this, the leader must broadcast its decision to the network once it get enough locks, and once the final decision is taken. Note that eager locking and the notification mechanism are only needed on synchronous collaborative work.

2.6   Classification of the Case Study

In Chap. 1, Villanueva et al. have introduced a classification for several case studies. According to their Table 1.1 TransDraw is really closed to the WallShare case study. The interface is not "Divisible" or "Distributable" because there are no interaction objects (IO) in two different interaction surfaces (IS). It can reach a unified state and has a divided state. Unlike WallShare, it is here possible to have all the ISs on the same platform. It has at least one distributed state because each IO can be in a different platform.

2.7   Conclusion and Future Work

We have seen that several synchronous collaborative applications are currently We have seen that several synchronous collaborative applications are currently based on centralized synchronization. This strategy is efficient but not fault-tolerant because it strongly relies on the stability of the server. Some applications achieve fault tolerance by replicating the state of the server, but this requires a more sophisticated infrastructure and it is still inherently centralized. Single point of control is a single point of failure.

We propose to implement these kind of applications on top of structured overlay networks with symmetric replication, and a transactional layer based on consensus.

This strategy provides synchronization and fault-tolerance by decentralizing the control of the work flow. We present our approach by taking the TransDraw application and the Beernet peer-to-peer network.

Beernet as is, can help to decentralize asynchronous collaborative applications. In order to achieve the functionality of TransDraw, which is synchronous, eager locking and a notification mechanism need to be added to the current transactional protocol.

We still need to study in detail the new transactional protocol, implement it and compare the performance with the centralized approach. We expect to have a small degradation in performance at the level of the transactional protocol due to replication cost, but with a huge gain in fault-tolerance. There is no degradation in performance for the user in case of no conflicts, because its changes are done optimistically, eliminating the problem of network latency.

Acknowledgments This work has been funded by the European Commission FP6 IST Project SELFMAN (Contract 034084), with support of the ITEA2-Call3-2008026 UsiXML European project.

References

1. Mejías, B. (2009). Beernet – the relaxed peer-to-peer network. http://beernet.info.ucl.ac.be.
2. Grolaux, D. (1998). Editeur graphique réparti basé sur un modèle transactionnel, 1998. Mémoire de Licence.
3. Pages, B. (2009). The bouml tool box. http://bouml.sourceforge.net.
4. 0x539 dev group. (2009). The gobby collaborative editor. http://gobby.0x539.de.
5. Gray, J., & Lamport, L. (2006). Consensus on transaction commit. *ACM Transactions on Database Systems, 31*(1), 133–160.
6. Google. (2009). Google docs. http://docs.google.com.
7. Mejías, B., & Van Roy, P. (2007). A relaxed-ring for self-organising and fault-tolerant peer-to-peer networks. *XXVI International Conference of the Chilean Computer Science Society, IEEE Computer Society* (November 2007).
8. Stoica, I., Morris, R., Karger, D., Kaashoek, F., & Balakrishnan, H. (2001). Chord: A scalable peer-to-peer lookup service for internet applications. *Proceedings of the 2001 ACM SIGCOMM Conference*, pp. 149–160.
9. Moser, M., & Haridi, S. (2007). Atomic commitment in transactional dhts. *Proceedings of the CoreGRID Symposium, CoreGRID series*, Springer.

Chapter 3
Distributed UI on Interactive Tabletops: Issues and Context Model

Sébastien Kubicki, Sophie Lepreux, and Christophe Kolski

Abstract The User Interface distribution can also be applied on interactive tabletops which are connected and more or less remote. This distribution raises issues which concern collaboration (how to distribute the UI to collaborate?); besides, concerning the tangible interaction: which role and appearance (tangible or virtual) must have the objects? In this chapter we describe an extended context model in order to take into account both interactions on a single interactive tabletop and interactions which are distributed and collaborative. The model proposed can, from our point of view, be used to make sure that the usability of the interaction is guaranteed. Indeed, it is essential to know the interaction configuration in order to ensure the usability of the system. The model suggested is illustrated in a case study integrating collaboration and UI distribution. A conclusion gives the limits of the article before a presentation of prospects.

3.1 Introduction

In a world in which everything and everybody are connected, it is possible to envisage connecting different platforms in order to carry out remote collaborations [1–4] (see also the chapters written by Garrido Navarro and his colleagues, Rädle

S. Kubicki (✉)
ENI Brest, UMR 6285, Lab-STICC, F-29200 Brest, France
e-mail: sebastien.kubicki@enib.fr

S. Lepreux • C. Kolski
Université Lille Nord de France, F-59000 Lille, France

UVHC, LAMIH, F-59313 Valenciennes, France

CNRS, UMR8201, F-59313 Valenciennes, France
e-mail: Sophie.Lepreux@univ-valenciennes.fr; Christophe.Kolski@univ-valenciennes.fr

M.D. Lozano et al. (eds.), *Distributed User Interfaces: Usability and Collaboration*, Human–Computer Interaction Series, DOI 10.1007/978-1-4471-5499-0_3, © Springer-Verlag London 2013

and his colleagues, Harboe and his colleagues in this book). Our work concentrates on the connection of interactive tabletops on which the users interact using tangible objects. There are few works in existence relating to connected tables. Very often, some complementary devices are introduced, such as in work of Yamashita et al. [5] which adds a videoconferencing system in order to support collaboration. In our work, we propose the use of one or several tables and some tangible objects in order to support interaction and collaboration. In [6], collaboration scenarios were presented according to different configurations (type of source platform and target platform, distribution strategy (master/slave or autonomous entities), UI distribution type (complete/partial), collaboration type (synchronous/asynchronous)). As suggested in Fig. 3.1, in case of inter-connected tabletops, problematics concerning centralized distribution of UI, as well as network of DUI are various; for instance: how to connect such interaction supports? How to duplicate and extract information? etc. [6]. Afterwards, in [1], a concept of tangible objects called *Tangigets* is defined and illustrated, making it possible to support distant collaboration between a tangible interactive tabletop and other surfaces. Considering that the context could be a means to ensure the system usability [7], we think that it is interesting to take the context into account in order to try to propose usable surfaces.

In this article we propose to use the context model suggested by Kubicki et al. [8, 9], which we widened so as to integrate the specificities of interactive tabletops in order then to widen it even further to integrate distribution characteristics. The following section of the article introduces the *TangiSense* interactive tabletop as well as the architecture which enables it to manage distribution. Then, we present the proposed context model. An application of this model is then illustrated before concluding and proposing research prospects.

3.2   From *TangiSense* Interactive Tabletop to Distributed Surfaces

This section aims to give a brief presentation of the support of our work which is the *TangiSense* interactive tabletop. This table has the characteristic of not being tactile, unlike the majority of interactive tabletops present on the market or in the scientific literature. It proposes a direct interaction via tangible objects. Table 3.1 presents eight different interactive tabletops, each one using a different capture technology.

It shows that each capture technology has its own characteristics. That is why the current interactive tabletops combine technologies. For more information, see Kubicki et al. [17].

The first part of this section presents the table while the second one presents the software architecture adopted to support the collaboration and the distribution between surfaces.

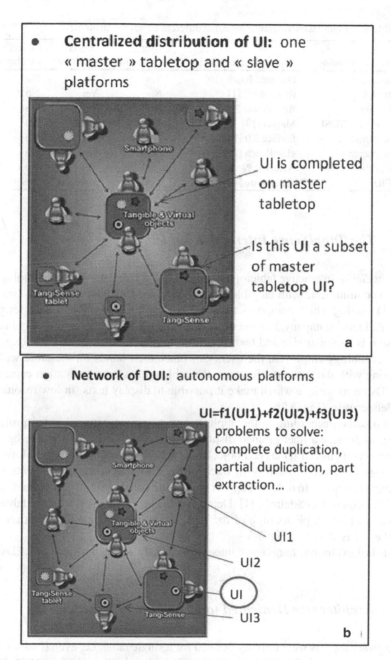

Fig. 3.1 Problematics concerning (**a**) centralized distribution of UI, (**b**) network of DUI

Table 3.1 Eight interactive tabletops using different capture technologies

Capture technology	Representative example	User distinction	Object detection	Object overlay
Capacitance	DiamondTouch [10]	Yes	No	No
Rear DI	ReacTable [11]	No	Yes	No
Webcam	Blip-Tronic 3000 [12]	No	Yes	No
Fiber optical/DSI	Magets [13]	No	Yes	No
PixelSense	Surface 2.0 [14]	No	Yes	No
Touchscreen	eLabBench [15]	No	Yes	No
Magnetic	Actuated Workbench [16]	No	Yes	No
RFID	*TangiSense* [17]	Yes	Yes	Yes

3.2.1 The TangiSense Interactive Tabletop

The *TangiSense* interactive tabletop is a prototype which uses RFID technology in order to communicate with tangible objects (equipped with RFID tag(s)). One tile of RFID reading which composes the table is shown in Fig. 3.2a. It was designed by the RFIdées[1] company. For the users, the tabletop looks like a traditional table, because it is a similar size and texture (glass) to a table for everyday use (e.g. due to the technology employed, the users can place their hands on the table without interfering with the system). However, the tabletop has communication capacities via LEDs on its surface which make it possible to display texts (in low resolution) or to define zones (Fig. 3.2b).

It is possible, according to the applications, to use an external video projector in order to provide a finer grained display and to project directly on tabletop. The tabletop detects the RFID tagged objects and reacts according to them. Moreover, RFID tags offer the possibility to track objects, to store data into objects or to superimpose objects. In order to support the remote collaboration, particular objects, named *Tangigets*, were defined [1]. Details on the technical aspects of the table can be found in [18]. A photograph of the table in an experimentation situation with several users is shown in Fig. 3.3.

In its last evolution, *TangiSense* integrates directly a screen instead of LEDs.

3.2.2 Architecture Dedicated to Distributed Interaction

The software aspects were initially defined for a single table, i.e. even if tables were physically connected, no interaction was envisaged with other platforms (the initial architecture is presented in Kubicki et al. [18]). From now on, the table architecture

---

[1]www.rfidees.fr

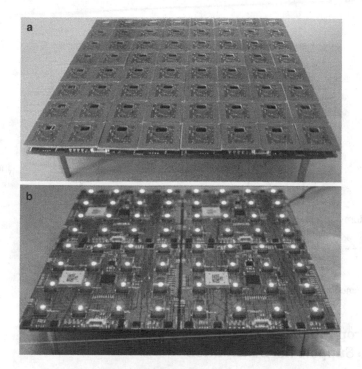

Fig. 3.2 Tiles composing the tabletop in its first versions

Fig. 3.3 *TangiSense*, its objects and users during experimentation

has evolved in order to be able to connect several tables and even several platforms, and so allow distribution [8, 19, 20]. This architecture Fig. 3.4 is based on a Multi-Agent System (MAS) which will make it possible to integrate the context adaptation rules. The architecture is fully described in [19] and allows us to consider new distributed interactions in various contexts.

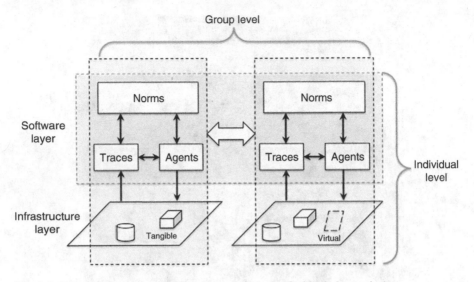

Fig. 3.4 Functional architecture of *TangiSense* [19] (case of tables in interaction)

3.3 Proposition of Context Interaction Model to Support the Distribution

Context-aware computing [21] appeared along with mobile platforms in order to adapt the applications to these new more restricted devices. In these contexts the user was alone on the platform but could switch from one platform to another (in general only one at the same time).[2] Since then, many definitions and evolutions have covered the concept of context awareness. However, we chose to base our work on the Calvary et al. [23] proposal which defines the context as a triplet <User, Platform, Environment>. From this triplet and a set of definitions from the state of the art, we proposed a context model [9]. This model was enriched to take into account the specificities of the interactive tabletops [8].

From a *User* point of view (Fig. 3.5), the most important modification in comparison to the other platforms is the **cardinality** between User and Platform. Indeed, the interactive tabletops make it possible to work with several users around their surface. The **Location** of the user relating to the platform is very important and influences the platform (display) itself. Indeed, the context will not be the same if the user *position* is on one side of the table (e.g. East) or on the opposite side (e.g. West). User *posture*, sitting or standing, is also important. Finally the interaction style is **Post-WIMP** and corresponds to competences in the use of tactile technology which can be *multiTouch* (**tactile interactions**), or in the

---

[2]However some works such as those of Grolaux et al. [22] are proposed on interface distribution between two types of platform.

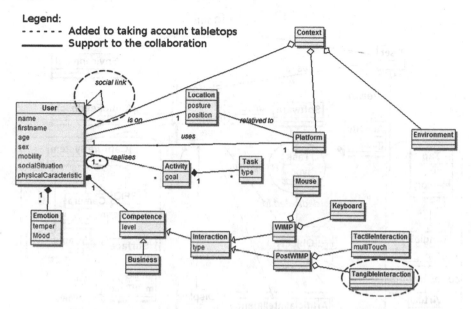

Fig. 3.5 . User-centric context-awareness model integrating the specifications for the interaction with interactive tabletops, collaboration and the distribution

use of objects (**tangible interaction**). The users who are collaborating together can have a **social link** which will influence their collaboration (parents/children, manager/employee, husband/wife, etc). It would also be necessary to specify which of the tasks are collaborative. It may only be a few of them (*partial* distribution) or all of them (*full* distribution). Problems appear concerning the distribution of the users distributed on tabletops: how to communicate, synchronize the tasks, collaborate? Some particular objects have to be defined to solve such problems [1].

From a *Platform* point of view (Fig. 3.6), an attribute was added making it possible to know if the platform is *multiUser* or not. In order to detect inconsistencies relating to the position of the user (criteria Location, attribute position), an attribute making it possible to know the *height* of the platform was added. One of the interactive tabletop's characteristics is also the capacity to recognize or interact with a set of **objects**. We distinguish two object *types*: **virtual** objects (which are generally video-projected or displayed) and **tangible** objects (physical objects placed on the table). From a general point of view, the tangible objects are equipped with **tags**. These tags can be of a different *type*: bar-codes, RFID, etc., often stuck under objects so as to enable their identification. According to the **capture system**, it is possible to vary the *number* of tags stuck under the object. Thus with three tags stuck under an object, it is possible, for example, to (re)form the shape of the object using software or to detect the direction of rotation of the object (e.g. in the case of RFID technology). The RFID Technology makes it possible to store information directly in the object. Thus the object has a *memory* enabling it to be completely independent from the table. In the case of virtual objects, it is a **videoprojector**

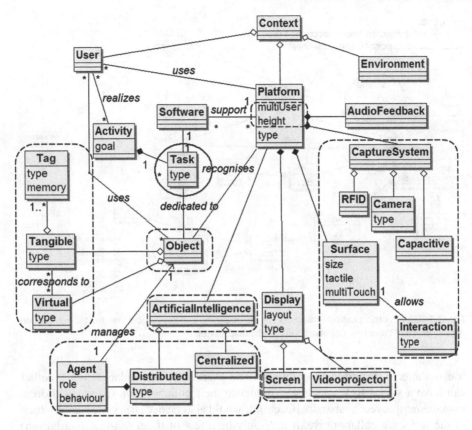

Fig. 3.6 Platform-centric context-awareness model integrating the specifications for the interaction with interactive tabletops, collaboration and the distribution

which is mainly used (it is the case with the first version of *TangiSense*). These platforms also evolve as regards the work **surface** and depend on the capture system. Finally, certain platforms can also carry an Artificial Intelligence element which can be centralized or distributed (e.g. *TangiSense*). A difficulty about the distribution is to connect many platforms, particularly when they have heterogenous characteristics: UI adaptation may bring promising solutions [8].

Concerning the Environment (Fig. 3.7), a criterion which was added relates to the collective classification of the environment: either (1) the users use the common part of the interactive tabletop, the type of workspace is then common; or (2) they use different parts of the tabletop, each one having their own workspace, in this case the type of workspace is individual [17].

In order to take the collaboration into account, a collaborative environment criterion was added to the Environment characteristics. Indeed, this is the environment conditions which will possibly lead the users to collaborate. This collaborative environment can be distinguished through two characteristics which will influence

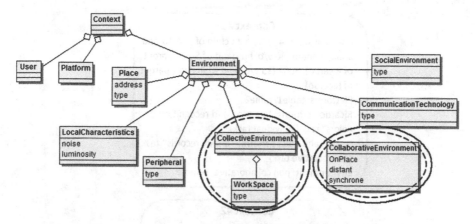

Fig. 3.7 Environment-centric context-awareness model integrating the specifications for the interaction with interactive tabletops, collaboration and the distribution

the interactions. Either the users collaborate by using the table (meaning a single table), in this case the collaboration is considered to be on site; or the collaboration is done on several distant platforms (the users use the table and at least one other distant support such as another table and/or another platform); in this case the environment is one of remote collaboration. The method of collaboration must be also added to the environment in order to know if collaboration is synchronous or asynchronous.

The next section aims to introduce a simulation to show our proposition and models in real context situations.

3.4 Simulation

The scenario involves a child working on an amusing activity on a first interactive tabletop: Ricardo performs one or several school exercises. In particular, he is currently using the "learning and recognition of colors" application.

This application intended to teach the recognition and learning of colors (only red, yellow, blue and green) to children (aged from 2 to 5 according to the level of difficulty). The scenario is based on the French teaching syllabus for nursery schools. We asked a teacher to imagine one or more scenarios using an interactive tabletop and a set of objects without giving any limits or constraints. The teacher proposed a simple application in which the children have to move a set of objects which have "lost their color" into the suitably colored frame (i.e. a "black and white" *bee* should be placed inside a yellow frame) [24].

Meanwhile, his parents, Renato and Sofia, interact in another room around a second interactive tabletop (used with another goal, such as family records). The human-machine interface is different on both platforms in this first context.

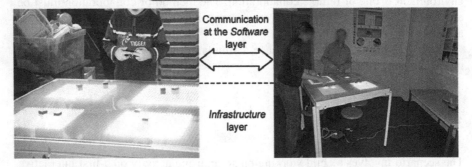

Context #1
- Users: Ricardo (4 years old ; child of Renato and Sofia), Renato (40 y/o, husband of Sofia, parent of Ricardo), Sofia (35 y/o, wife of Renato, parent of Ricardo)
- Platforms: table1, table2
- Ricardo performs: "learning and recognition of colors" task (individual task)
- Renato and Sofia perform: "family records" task (collaborative task)
- Environment: non collaborative, remote

Context #2
- Users: no change
- Platforms: no change
- Ricardo performs: "learning and recognition of colors" task (collaborative task)
- Renato and Sofia perform: "learning and recognition of colors" (collaborative task)
- Environment: collaborative, remote

Communication at the *Software* layer

Infrastructure layer

Fig. 3.8 Illustration of the users in remote collaboration (context #2)

The child may at various times request assistance (remote collaboration) from his parents. They must be based on a common support to facilitate collaboration (e.g. direct or indirect advice to be provided on the color of certain vegetables): the human-machine interface must be distributed on the two tabletops in this second context.

An illustration is provided in Fig. 3.8. Several attributes of the context have changed, leading to the adaptation of the distributed interaction.

Such situations are under study and development. Different evaluations are also planned.

3.5 Conclusion and Prospects

This chapter has presented the *TangiSense* tabletop and its software architecture. This architecture allows UI distribution between different tabletops and surfaces in general. This distribution is possible by integrating the intelligence of the distribution in the agents of a multi-agent system (developed with JADE [25]). Then a global context model has been described; it has been extended by taking the specificities of tabletops into account. The context model proposed in this chapter considers UI distribution on surfaces.

Our research perspectives are the following: to propose a set of adaptation mechanisms integrated into the multi-agent systems, based on the context model proposed; to propose explicit relations between the context model and usability criteria; to validate progressively the context model in various experiments, including remote collaboration.

Acknowledgments This research work was partially financed by the "Ministère de l'Education Nationale, de la Recherche et de la Technologie", the "région Nord Pas de Calais", the "Centre National de la Recherche Scientifique", the FEDER, CISIT, and especially the "Agence Nationale de la Recherche" (ANR TTT and IMAGIT projects ANR 2010 CORD 01701). The authors thank also Yoann Lebrun, Emmanuel Adam and René Mandiau for their contribution in this research.

References

1. Lepreux, S., Kubicki, S., Kolski, C., & Caelen, J. (2012). From centralized interactive tabletops to distributed surfaces: The tangiget concept. *International Journal of Human-Computer Interaction, 28*, 709–721.
2. Vanderdonckt, J. (2010). Distributed user interfaces: How to distribute user interface elements across users, platforms, and environments. Keynote address, *Proceedings of the International Conference on Interaccion*.
3. Gallud, J. A., Tesoriero, R., & Penichet, V. M. R. (Eds.). (2011). *Distributed user interfaces, designing interfaces for the distributed ecosystem*. London: Springer. ISBN 978-1-4471-2270-8.
4. Tesoriero, R., & Lozano, M. D. (2012). Distributed user interfaces: Applications and challenges. *International Journal of Human-Computer Interaction, 28*(11), 697–699.
5. Yamashita, N., Kuzuoka, H., Hirata, K., Aoyagi, S., & Shirai, Y. (2011). Supporting fluid tabletop collaboration across distances. *Proceedings of CHI'11, ACM*. Vancouver, pp. 2827–2836.
6. Lepreux, S., Kubicki, S., Kolski, C., & Caelen, J. (2011). A step towards the distribution of tangible and virtual objects. In J. A. Gallud, R. Tesoriero, & V. R. Penichet (Eds.), *Distributed user interfaces* (pp. 133–143). New York: Springer. ISBN 978-1-4471-2270-8.
7. Yang, S., Lu, Y., Gupta, S., & Cao, Y. (2012). Does context matter? The impact of use context on mobile internet adoption. *International Journal of Human-Computer Interaction, 28*(8), 530–541.
8. Kubicki, S., Lebrun, Y., Lepreux, S., Adam, E., Kolski, C., & Mandiau, R. (2013). Simulation in contexts involving an interactive table and tangible objects. *Simulation Modelling Practice and Theory, 31*, 116–131.
9. Kubicki, S. (2011). Contribution à la prise en considération du contexte dans la conception de tables interactives sous l'angle de l'IHM, application à des contextes impliquant table interactive RFID et objets tangibles. Ph.D. thesis, Université de Valenciennes, France.

10. Dietz, P., & Leigh, D. (2001). DiamondTouch: A multiuser touch technology. *Proceedings of UIST'01* (pp. 219–226). ACM Press, Orlando.
11. Jordà, S., Kaltenbrunner, M., Geiger, G., & Alonso, M. (2006). The reacTable: A tangible tabletop musical instrument and collaborative workbench. *Proceedings of SIGGRAPH'06.* ACM, New York, p. 91.
12. Benett, P., Toru, S., & Tutte-Scali, L. (2005). Blip-Tronic 3000. http://www.petecube.com/bliptronic3000
13. Weiss, M., Schwarz, F., Jakubowski, S., & Borchers, J. (2010). Madgets: Actuating widgets on interactive tabletops. In *UIST'10: 23nd Annual ACM Symposium on User Interface Software and Technology.* New York, pp. 293–302.
14. How does pixelsense work? (Online). http://www.microsoft.com/en-us/pixelsense/pixelsense.aspx
15. http://www.microsoft.com/surface/, 2011.
16. Pangaro, G., Maynes-Aminzade, D., & Ishii, H. (2002). The actuated workbench: Computer-controlled actuation in tabletop tangible interfaces. *Proceedings of UIST'02.* ACM, pp. 181–190.
17. Kubicki, S., Lepreux, S., & Kolski, C. (2011). RFID-driven situation awareness on TangiSense, a table interacting with tangible objects. *Personal and Ubiquitous Computing, 16*(8), 1079–1094.
18. Kubicki, S., Lepreux, S., Lebrun, Y., Santos, P. D., Kolski, C., & Caelen, J. (2009). New human-computer interactions using tangible objects: Application on a digital tabletop with RFID technology. In J. A. Jacko (Ed.), *Human-Computer Interaction* (LNCS, Vol. 5612, pp. 446–455). New York: Springer.
19. Garbay, C., Badeig, F., & Caelen, J. (2012). Normative multi-agent approach to support collaborative work in distributed tangible environments. *Proceedings of CSCW'12,* Seattle.
20. Lebrun, Y., Adam, E., Kubicki, S., & Mandiau, R. (2010). A multi-agent system approach for interactive table using RFID. In Y. Demazeau, F. Dignum, J. M. Corchado, & J. B. Perez (Eds.), *8th International Conference on Practical Applications of Agents and Multi-agent Systems (PAAMS 2010),* Springer. Advances in Intelligent and Soft-Computing, Advances in Practical Applications of Agents and Multiagent Systems, Vol. 70, (pp. 125–134). ISBN:978-3-642-12383-2.
21. Schilit, B., Adams, N., & Want, R. (1994). Context-aware computing applications. *WMCSA'94: Workshop on Mobile Computing Systems and Applications* (pp. 85–90). IEEE Press, Santa Cruz.
22. Grolaux, D., Vanderdonckt, J., & Van Roy, P. (2005). Attach me, detach me, assemble me like you work. In M. Costabile & F. Paterno (Eds.), *Human-computer interaction INTERACT 2005* (Vol. 3585, pp. 198–212). Berlin/Heidelberg: Springer.
23. Calvary, G., Demeure, A., Coutaz, J., & Dâassi, O. (2004). Adaptation des interfaces homme-machine à leur contexte d'usage. *Revue D'intelligence Artificielle, 18*(4), 577–606.
24. Kubicki, S., Lepreux, S., & Kolski, C. (2011). Evaluation of an interactive table with tangible objects: Application with children in a classroom. In *2nd Workshop on Child Computer Interaction "UI Technologies and Educational Pedagogy",* at *CHI'2011,* Vancouver.
25. Bellifemine, F., Poggi, A., & Rimassa, G. (2001). Developing multi-agent systems with a FIPA-compliant agent framework. *Software Practice and Experience, 31*(2), 103–128.

Chapter 4
Collaborative Content Creation Using Web-Based Distributed User Interface (DUI)

Yong-Moo Kwon, Changhyeon Lee, and Fathoni Arief Musyaffa

Abstract This paper describes collaborative social authoring technology using web-based distributed user interface (DUI). In view of collaboration, web is one of the most common user environments on various systems of desktop and mobile devices. This paper addresses the DUI issues for the support of multiple kind of devices, such as PC, smartphone, tablet and so on. Our system defines CAM (Collaborative Authoring Metadata) for collaborative authoring in distributed environment. The CAM is used for the exchange of authoring intention of each user during the collaborative authoring. Several elements of CAM are defined, which are useful for exchanging information among distributed users. Our system also provides the recommendation engine for referring and adding the related contents media from the participants' social media services account during the authoring process.

4.1 Introduction

This paper addresses the issues on developing web-based collaborative content authoring in multi-device environment and utilizing metadata provided in uploaded media, as well as providing social contents recommendation using metadata provided in the user's Facebook account. Our proposed system is considering a distributed user interfaces (DUIs) [1] for collaborative authoring, which is based on the concept of UI component adequate for the physical device characteristics and social media recommendation scheme from SNS such as Facebook.

This paper describes our approach for web-based social collaborative authoring technology and shows some current research results.

Y.-M. Kwon (✉) • C. Lee • F.A. Musyaffa
KIST, 39-1 Hawalgogdong Sungbukku, Seoul, Korea
e-mail: ymk@kist.re.kr; pott183b@imrc.kist.re.kr; fathoni@imrc.kist.re.kr

M.D. Lozano et al. (eds.), *Distributed User Interfaces: Usability and Collaboration*,
Human–Computer Interaction Series, DOI 10.1007/978-1-4471-5499-0_4,
© Springer-Verlag London 2013

39

Consider some memorable events such as wedding ceremony, high school graduation or academic fair that involves a group of friends who took photos at the event. Each friend took a photo based on their own perspective and their own point of interest. Each friend tends to have different interest, so photographs taken by different friends will likely cover the event from different perspectives. Hence, collecting the photos from various sources is needed to comprehend the whole event from various perspectives. The resulting photos also tend to be distributed in each photographer's personal drive. It is cumbersome to obtain their photos one by one. And then, to obtain friends' multimedia, each user uses own device. At this point, each user may use various kinds of devices. Some of the users use desktop in their home and office. However, some of the users use mobile devices for publishing their multimedia and obtaining their friends' multimedia from SNS.

Fortunately, the widespread usage of SNS helps photo sharing among friends. Using the photo content uploaded in the SNS, the users can collaboratively combine the photos to create a video content that has personal meaning. To create narrative video using photos on a certain event, the authors need related photo content about certain topic/event to support content authoring. However, to our best knowledge, no current authoring tools support recommending media content from SNS, such as Facebook. An SNS-based content recommendation system for authoring is needed in our collaborative authoring system.

The goal for developing recommendation system is to help the collaborating authors by providing related photos from Facebook. The recommendation module is a novel method for video authoring. The recommendation module suggests related photos from SNS based on the keyword in the analyzed Collaborative Authoring Metadata (CAM) [2].

Kaplan and Heinlein [3] categorized social media into various types, including Social Networking Services (SNSs). The content in SNS has deeper social meaning than content-communities social media, because it has higher self-presentation and self-disclosure. One of the most popular SNS is Facebook. Statistics presented by Hachman [4] claims that Facebook has 901 million users. Parr [5] reported that 250 million photos are uploaded every day on Facebook. The photo uploaded in SNS (e.g. Facebook) tends to be much more personal and have deeper social relationship meaning compared to content community social media (e.g. Flickr). For this reason, in view of social collaborative authoring, Facebook's photo contents are prominent resources for the content being authored due to the amount of contents it contains and the social relationship meaning of the contents to the users. The next challenge is how to recommend related photo contents to the authoring system.

Mobile devices are currently widely used. In a January 2012 statistics provided by Ansonalex.com, there are 5 billion mobile phones used worldwide, and 1 billion of them are smartphone. Therefore, the usage of mobile devices to support daily activities is likely increasing, including the usage for collaborative purpose.

As DUI application, this paper describes the development of Facebook photo recommendation for collaborative social video User Created Content (UCC) authoring tool. Several things are done to achieve this goal, such as (a) Studying the behavior of Facebook users in sharing photo content to their Facebook account, and (b) Designing and implementing recommendation mechanism for getting co-event content from Facebook and prioritizing the result.

This paper also describes collaborative method between mobile users and desktop users. Mobile users can be recommended multimedia from SNS and participate collaborative authoring via web environment. Current mobile devices have a rich set of features, such as GPS, camera, microphone, wireless networks (Bluetooth, Wifi, 3G, LTE) with decent computational resources. In view of collaboration, mobile device advantages can be used to support collaboration. The users can support content creation by doing one of the authoring tasks: video authoring, audio authoring, and image authoring. The users can support content authoring by providing various multimodal contents, such as video, audio, image and even text. In our system, user can participate in collaborative authoring task with their friends which use various kinds of devices.

4.2   Related Work

There are many researches on collaborative authoring [6–13] and collaborative softwares [14] that support various purposes. Among them, the typical web-based document collaboration tools are Google Docs and Wiki. The Google Docs provides simultaneous document editing; however there is lack of communication to share the editing intention. The Wiki has a lack of contents sharing during authoring process and also lack of group management between authors.

In 2011, the Creaza VideoCloud Platform is introduced [15], which is a tool for collaborative video authoring on the web. Lately, this tool is called as WeVideo [16] as a commercial solution. The main feature of WeVideo includes web-based collaboration, video authoring, and utilization of cloud. However, WeVideo is lack of communication to share collaborating the editing intention and comments among collaborative authors.

Stupeflix [17] is a web application to make videos in a few clicks. This solution imports directly from Facebook, Flickr, Picasa or Dropbox. User can add text, maps, voice-over, images and videos. This one also provides customized preview and free videos for download in HD. Stupeflix provides open API for developers. This solution provides open APIs for developers. This solution does not support collaborative authoring; however, it supports the coordination with SNS (social network services) contents for video authoring.

4.3   Collaborative Contents Creation Using Web-Based Distributed User Interfaces

Our general direction can be seen in Fig. 4.1. The users have multiple devices (e.g. tablets, smartphones, PCs and notebooks) with different display size, computational resource, and features. Every devices connected to the internet, and the

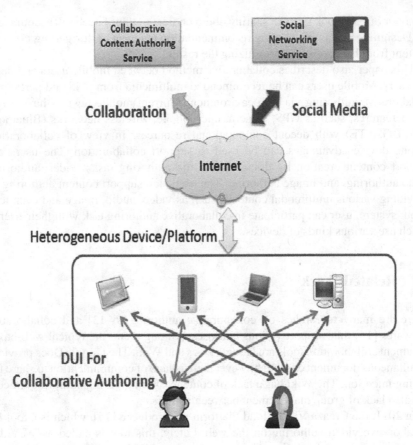

Fig. 4.1 General direction of the proposed system

internet connects the users to several services, such as mobile messaging service, collaborative content authoring service, and social networking service. The users can create a content using web based collaborative authoring service anywhere, using any devices that connected through the internet. Since the user might not feel convenient using the UI developed for desktop in their mobile devices, component based specific UI for mobile devices are developed.

In view of DUIs, for heterogeneous device/platform, a concept of UI component is used and its component can be downloaded to devices according to the authoring purpose and device's physical characteristics. In other words, functionalities of collaborative authoring can be divided into component. For example, the authoring of multimedia contents handles several media, such as image, video, audio and text. In the desktop environment, the authoring tool provides all the functionalities for multimedia in one application UI. However, in case of mobile devices, it is not possible to provide all multimedia authoring functionalities in mobile device with small screen and low computational capability.

Another consideration is the authoring system did not have the capability of adapting the UI according to specific editing part for the user. Some authors might be expert to provide audio enhancements on the project (audio authoring), while the other authors are excellent in narrative visual storytelling (video authoring), and the other users might know many things that could be used to provide textual information on the project (textual authoring). In this case, it is needed to provide adaptability of the interface based on the users' intention (or expertise). For supporting the expertise in collaboration, our system supports three interfaces, Audio Authoring User Interface, Video Authoring User Interface, and Textual Authoring User Interface.

Collaborative work needs to share knowledge, experience and abilities to achieve common goals among users. It is important to share user's characteristics for collaborative authoring on distributed environment among users. For collaborative authoring, our system designed CAM (Collaborative Authoring Metadata) that includes authoring intention, name of author, created date, time, location, mood, with whom and so on. Each of users can upload and create their own contents (Video, Image, Audio and Text) to collaborative authoring space. When user upload and create their own contents, CAM is created as additional knowledge and experience.

It should be noted that although there are personally meaningful multimedia data in our social networking sites; the current authoring tools are incapable of recommending multimedia contents from our social networking sites, such as Facebook. This paper addresses the issue of the related contents recommendation from social media services during the collaborative authoring. The above mentioned CAM is used for the recommendation of social media contents.

4.4   Recommendation Technique Review

For the contents authoring, the recommendation of appropriate related contents are needed. Recommender system is a software tool and technique that suggests items to be used by a user [18–20]. The term "Item" refers to what the system recommends to users. In most cases, a recommendation system only focuses on a specific type of item (e.g., movies, news or music). In the past few years, recommendation system has become a valuable means to cope with the problem of information overload [21].

The interest towards recommender systems has been dramatically increased lately, as indicated by some facts. First, recommender systems play an important role in such highly rated internet sites (e.g. IMDb, Amazon.com). Second, there are dedicated conferences and workshops related to the recommendation system field (e.g. ACM Recommender Systems – RecSys). Third, college courses that dedicated entirely to recommendation system are offered at higher education institutions around the world. Lastly, there have been several special issues in academic journals that cover research and developments about recommendation system [21].

Recommendation systems have several differences with search engines. The goal of search engine is to answer user's ad hoc queries, while recommender systems are created to recommend services or items to user. The input of a search engine is defined as a query, while recommendation systems also rely on user preferences that defined as a profile. Output of a search engine is ranked items relevant to user's need, meanwhile, in recommendation systems, the items are ranked based on user's preferences. Search engines rely mainly in information retrieval-based methods, while recommendation systems rely on several methods, such as information retrieval, machine learning, and user modeling [22].

There are two major approaches for recommendation systems. First, collaborative filtering based recommendation systems as described by Goldberg et al. [23], and Second, content-based filtering based recommendation systems as explained by Pazzani and Billsus [24]. Collaborative filtering uses data from another user with similar preferences (e.g. Amazon.com's item recommendation). Collaborative filtering-based recommendation systems identify users whose preferences are similar to the current user and recommend items that have been liked by identified users [25]. Meanwhile, content-based filtering is based on the description of the item and a profile of user's interest (e.g. Internet Movie Database movie recommendation). Content-based filtering-based recommendation system tries to recommend similar item to those a given user has liked in the past [25]. Some works use tags as content descriptors for collaborative filtering, such as work by Firan et al. [26] shows that tag-based profile is capable of producing better personal recommendations on Last.fm compared to conventional recommendations. Meanwhile, Guy et al. [27] use related people and related tags to recommend social media items (blogs, communities, wikis, bookmarks, files) using hybrid approach (both collaborative filtering and content-based filtering). After evaluating the result, they found that tag-based recommendation provides better item recommendation, and recommendation based on combination of people and tags provides slightly more interesting recommendation with less already-known items.

Lerman et al. [28] worked on recommendation system that tried to solve ambiguity caused by homonyms and polysemy in Flickr tags. Their work uses hybrid approach (combining collaborative filtering and content-based filtering) based in contacts and tags. Recommendation based on users' contacts has proven to significantly improve the relevancy. In tag based part, a probabilistic topic model that predicts the users' desired contexts is developed. The probabilistic topic model is based on previous tags used by the user and to which group the user assigns his/her photos into. The result for this is a model that interprets the keyword as intended by the user (not biased by either homonym or polysemy). Thus, the precision of recommended item increased. In this work, comment and favorites were not utilized and there was no way to handle uninformative tags (e.g. "Let's Play"). Gursel and Sen [29] proposed another recommendation system which is also based on Flickr. They developed an agent that observes the user's past activities and observes rating and comments provided by the user. As a result, photos are recommended in order, based on user preferences. Unfortunately, user with lack of past activities may have irrelevant agent. And also, the content source is derived from Flickr, therefore may not have a deep social meaning compared to SNS websites like Facebook.

4.5   Results

4.5.1   Our Social Collaborative Authoring System

This paper describes an architecture which can support the concept of DUI and links with SNS, such as Facebook. This architecture is provided in Fig. 4.2.

The proposed system consists of web-based DUIs, web server and social database.

Web-based DUI provides a space to create project of collaborative authoring, publish the content, and manage authors' accounts. In more detail, AUI (Authoring User Interface) is developed for desktop PC and mobile devices. Authors can store their resources (audio, photos, and videos), CAMs and friend's information in the social DB. The web server links web based DUI and social DB, and includes the modules for collaborative authoring system.

Web-based DUI can be composed according to the user's device. In case of desktop PC, user can use web browser in which all the authoring functionalities are provided. However, in case of mobile devices, user can select the DUI component

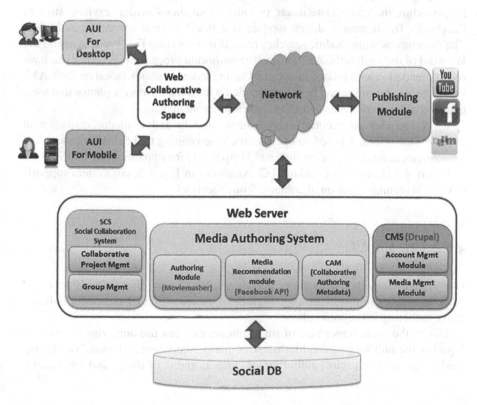

Fig. 4.2 Architecture of the social collaborative authoring system

according to the user intention. For example, the audio authoring user can only download the audio AUI and perform the collaborative authoring. Here, the pre-authored video and text content are provided as a reference in the timeline.

The web server consists of SCS (Social Collaborative System), MAS (Media Authoring System) and CMS (Contents Management System). The SCS includes collaborative project management module and group management module. These modules implement collaborative functions on the web. When a user searches for co-authors, group management module requests author's information at the social DB and provides appropriate author information to the requesting user. The collaborative project management manages group of the project.

The MAS includes authoring module, recommendation module and CAM module. The authoring module provides editing capability and preview of edited content. The CAM module creates CAM, analyzes created CAM and displays this CAM information systematically for collaborative authoring. Using these CAMs, authors can exchange their authoring intention and information of each media. CAM is provided by authors during media (image, video or audio) upload. Our system defines and stores CAM using XML.

In case of creating narrative story using images, the authors need related images or videos about certain topic. Our recommendation system can help the authors by providing the appropriate image or video from social media services, such as Facebook. The recommendation module is a novel method for media authoring. The recommendation module searches related images from Facebook based on the keyword of the analyzed CAM. During the authoring process, each author can have recommendation with related images and sound from Facebook based on the CAM. For example, the author can be recommended with some Facebook photos that were taken by other participants, which include similar metadata.

CMS includes an account management module and a media management module. Our system is based on open source video editing tool (Moviemasher [30]) for implementing authoring module and Drupal [31] for implementing CMS.

Figure 4.3 shows UI of desktop PC. As shown in Fig. 4.3, our system supports CAM and recommendation of contents from Facebook.

4.5.2   Mobile UI

Our system supports collaborative authoring using smart phone like iPhone and Android phone using web browser. Figure 4.4 shows whole UI menus for collaborative authoring in the smart phone.

Due to the small screen size of smart phone, user can use authoring component based on the authoring media, like image or audio. According to the user's authoring media type, user can select authoring UI, such as audio, or image and download it

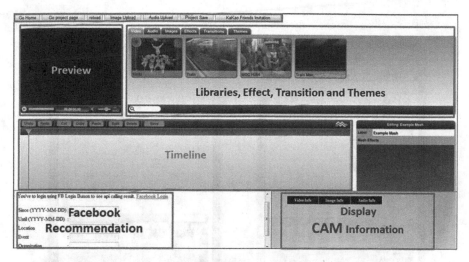

Fig. 4.3 Collaborative authoring tool for desktop PC

Fig. 4.4 Web app for collaborative video authoring

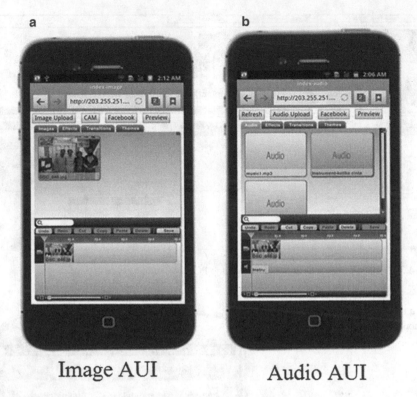

Fig. 4.5 Image and audio authoring user interface for smartphone. (a) Image AUI. (b) Audio AUI

in his/her smartphone. Then, he/she can perform collaborative authoring only in its authoring media UI. Figure 4.5 shows image authoring UI and audio authoring UI.

4.5.3 Invitation of Friends for Collaborative Authoring

For supporting collaborative authoring, our system supports friend or expert invitation in the authoring software. Figure 4.6 shows friend/expert invitation UI. Here, KakaoTalk, widely used message system, is used for sending invitation message and corresponding URL. When friend/expert received an invitation message, he/she can join the collaborative authoring simply by clicking the received message which links to an URL of web authoring space.

Fig. 4.6 Expert friend
invitation UI

4.5.4   CAM and Facebook Photo Metadata

This paper also addresses the coordination of our collaborative authoring system
and current Social Network Services such as Facebook, Flickr etc.

In Facebook, each user has many friends and shares several kinds of contents
with one's friends. So, for creating collaborative UCC, it would be also useful to
use our friend's Facebook album as a social database. For this, our system provides
coordination of our collaborative authoring system and Facebook photo album.

Here, participants' Facebook photos are accessed using Facebook API.

Our system supports the collaborative authoring based on the CAM. In Facebook
album, each photo can have several metadata information such as time, location,
likes, tagged person, comments and so on. So, these metadata of Facebook photo
can be used as CAM for our collaborative authoring. Using these Facebook photo
metadata, our system can search and collect the related photos of our friends from
Facebook album and create social UCC using these searched photos.

Figure 4.7 shows an example of CAM created by users. According to the user's
situation and state of mind, the CAM can be created differently. For example, user1
creates upper CAM (a) and user2 creates lower CAM (b) in Fig. 4.7. As shown in
the Fig. 4.7, user1 and user2 attended same event that is held at the same place.
However, they have different feeling and spend event with different friends. Our
system can use these different CAMs in collaborative work among distributed users.
These CAM can be used appropriately for the collaborative contents authoring.

Figure 4.8 shows a basic concept of recommendation system based on CAM. Our
system includes Facebook contents recommendation engine using CAM. The detail
of our recommendation engine will be described in another paper.

a

```
<image>
    <filename>DSC_048.jpg</filename>
    <date_created>2012-04-21</date_created>
    <mood>enjoy</mood>
    <weather>warm</weather>
    <location>Seoul</location>
    <with whom>Fidel Aja, Iwa Nurgadar</with_whom>
    <event>ICE</event>
    <organization>KIST</organization>
    <date>2012-04-24</date>
    <time> 02:44:08</time>
</image>
```

b

```
<image>
    <filename>DSC_033.jpg</filename>
    <date_created>2012-04-21</date_created>
    <mood>sad</mood>
    <weather>sunny</weather>
    <location>Seoul</location>
    <with whom>Hoang Phong, Hoang Hoa</with_whom>
    <event>ICE</event>
    <organization>KIST</organization>
    <date>2012-05-10</date>
    <time> 12:09:04</time>
</image>
```

Fig. 4.7 Examples of CAM created by two users

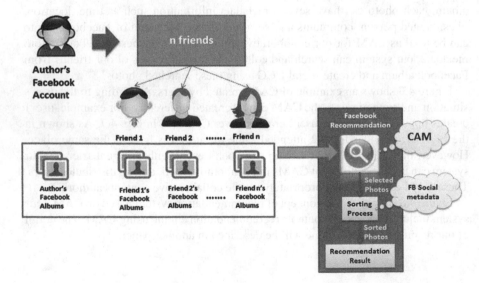

Fig. 4.8 Facebook recommendation scheme with CAM

4.6 Conclusions

This paper describes DUI issue for developing web-based user interface into collaborative social authoring. Our system provides web-based collaborative media editing environment and adopts CAM to communicate authoring intention and comments among collaborative authors, then coordinates with Facebook photo album. Our system addresses issues that arises in multi device authoring and proposes DUI for collaborative authoring, which has adaptability of the system to be used in multiple platforms and space.

Our system also introduces content recommendation scheme from Facebook during the collaborative authoring. The recommendation system for Facebook photos is developed by using several metadata available on Facebook. Content-based filtering and Collaborative Filtering is done sequentially to provide the recommendation. Instead of only using relevancy with the context, some social parameters like how close the relationship of the uploader to the user and how many interaction on a photo is measured to determine how interesting a photo is. Hence, it can provide relevant recommendation to be used as content resource for video authoring. After this work has done, web-based collaborative video authoring environment has developed and CAM has been adapted to match with social metadata available in Facebook. User can refer to CAM information to seek content recommendation from Facebook with a good accuracy from various perspective of the content to be authored, and based on this content; they can create content using relevant photo recommendation result.

Nowadays, the social curation technique is receiving much interest in view of collecting and reorganizing social contents in distributed and heterogeneous SNSes environment. Currently, we are now developing storytelling system using social curation technique. The future research issues include how to collect and group the SNS contents from distributed and heterogeneous SNS contents and how to provide collaborative storytelling system by using distributed multi-devices.

Acknowledgements This work is supported by "Development of Tangible Social Media Platform Technology" of KIST.

References

1. Niklas Elmqvist. (2011). Distributed user interfaces: state of the art. *CHI 2011 Workshop*.
2. Lee, C., & Kwon, Y. M. (2012). *Web based collaborative authoring technology for tangible social media*. Seattle: IWCES.
3. Kaplan, M., & Haenlein, A. M. (2010). Users of the world, unite! The challenges and opportunities of social media. *Business Horizons, 53*(1), 59–68.
4. Hachman, M. (2012). Facebook now totals 901 million users, profits slip http://www.pcmag.com/article2/0,2817,2403410,00.asp. Posted 23 Apr 2012.
5. Parr, B. (2011). Infographic. Facebook by the numbers. http://mashable.com/2011/10/21/facebook-infographic/. Posted 21 Oct 2011.

6. Joe Thurbon. (2010). Collaborative authoring. Intersect Australia Ltd.
7. Adler, A., Nash, J. C. & Noël, S. (2004). Challenges in collaborative authoring software. *Submitted to a Special Issue of the IEEE Transactions on Professional Communication "Expanding the boundaries of E-collaboration"*.
8. William Emigh, & Susan C. Herring. (2005). Collaborative authoring on the web: A genre analysis of online encyclopedias. *Proceedings of the 38th Hawaii International Conference on System Sciences*.
9. Mike Alcok. (2008). *Collaborative authoring – The future of e-learning*. Atlantic Link.
10. Thom-Santelli, J., Cosley, D., & Gay, G. (2009). *What's mine is mine: Territoriality in collaborative authoring*. Boston: CHI.
11. Ilaria Liccardi. (2010). Improving users' awareness interactions in the collaborative document authoring process: The CAWS approach. Ph.D. thesis, University of Southampton.
12. Changyan Chi, Michelle X. Zhou, Min Yang, Wenpeng Xiao, Yiqin Yu, & Xiaohua Sun. (2010). Dandelion: Supporting coordinated, collaborative authoring in Wikis. *CHI 2010*, 10–15 Apr 2010.
13. Yuanling Li, Paul Logasa Bogen II, Daniel Pogue, Richard Furuta, & Frank Shipman. (2012). Collaborative authoring of Walden's paths. *TPDL 2012*, LNCS 7489.
14. http://en.wikipedia.org/wiki/Collaborative_software
15. Takhirov, N., & Duchateau, F. (2011). A cloud-based and social authoring tool for video. *DocEng'11*, Mountain View.
16. WeVideo. http://www.wevideo.com/
17. Stupeflix. http://studio.stupeflix.com/en/
18. Mahmood, T., & Ricci, F. (2009). Improving recommender systems with adaptive conversational strategies. In C. Cattuto, G. Ruffo, F. Menczer (Eds.), *Hypertext* (pp. 73–82). ACM.
19. Resnick, P., & Varian, H. R. (1997). Recommender systems. *Communications of the ACM, 40*(3), 56–58.
20. Burke, R. (2007). Hybrid web recommender systems. In *The AdaptiveWeb* (pp. 377–408). Berlin/Heidelberg: Springer.
21. Ricci, F., Rokach, L., & Saphira, B. (2010). Introduction to recommender systems handbook. In F. Ricci, L. Rokach, B. Saphira, & P. B. Kantor (Eds.), *Recommender systems handbook* (pp. 1–29). New York: Springer.
22. Shaphira, B., & Rokach, L. (2012). Recommender systems and search engines – Two sides of the same coin? Slide Lecture. http://medlib.tau.ac.il/teldan-2010/bracha.ppt.
23. Goldberg, D., Nichols, D., Oki, B. M., & Terry, D. (1992). Using collaborative filtering to weave an information tapestry. *Communications of the ACM, 35*(12), 61–70.
24. Pazzani, M. J., & Billsus, D. (2007). Content-based recommendation systems. In P. Brusilovsky, A. Kobsa, & W. Neidl (Eds.), *The adaptive web: Methods and strategies of web personalization* (LNCS, Vol. 4321, pp. 325–341). Heidelberg: Springer.
25. Balabanovic, M., & Shoham, Y. (1997). Fab: Content-based, collaborative recommendation. *Communications of the ACM, 40*(3), 66–72.
26. Firan, C. S., Nejdl, W., & Paiu R. (2007). The benefit of using tag-based profiles. LA-WEB '07 *Proceedings of the 2007, Latin American Web Conference* (pp. 32–41). Washington, DC.
27. Guy, I., Zwerdling, N., Ronen, I., Carmel, D., & Uziel, E. (2010). *Social media recommendation based on people and tags* (pp. 194–201). New York: SIGIR.
28. Lerman, K., Plangprasopchok, A., & Wong, C. (2007). Personalizing image search results on flickr. In *AAAI workshop on Intelligent Techniques for Web Personalization*.
29. Gursel, A., & Sen, S. (2009). Improving search in social networks by agent based mining. *Ijcai'09 Proceedings of The 21st International Joint Conference on Artificial Intelligence* (pp. 2034–2039). San Francisco.
30. MovieMasher. http://www.moviemasher.com/
31. Drupal. http://drupal.org/

Chapter 5
TwisterSearch: A Distributed User Interface for Collaborative Web Search

Roman Rädle, Hans-Christian Jetter, and Harald Reiterer

Abstract Although a Web search is typically regarded as a solitary activity, collaborative search approaches are becoming an increasingly relevant topic for HCI and distributed user interfaces (DUIs). Today's collaborative search systems lack comprehensive search support that also involves pre- or post-search activities such as preparing for a search or making sense of search results. We believe that post-WIMP DUIs can help to better support social searches and have identified four design goals that are critical for their successful design. In consequence, we present TwisterSearch, an interactive DUI prototype that meets our four design goals. A formative study conducted with students at a high school shows its general applicability for educational purposes.

5.1 Introduction

In the recent years, research in HCI has increasingly focused on collaborative searches [1–6]. Collaborative search approaches can support activities and decision making such as planning travel, purchasing products, or searching for literature and could become important tools for users' information practice in future. Consequentially, Morris identified a great need for better tool support for collaborative Web searches [7].

We believe that distributed user interfaces (DUI) as defined by Elmqvist [8] are particularly appropriate for supporting collaborative Web searches, especially

R. Rädle (✉) • H. Reiterer
Human-Computer Interaction Group, University of Konstanz, Konstanz, Germany
e-mail: roman.raedle@uni-konstanz.de; harald.reiterer@uni-konstanz.de

H.-C. Jetter
Intel Collaborative Research Institute for Sustainable Connected Cities (ICRI Cities),
University College London, London, UK
e-mail: h.jetter@ucl.ac.uk

M.D. Lozano et al. (eds.), *Distributed User Interfaces: Usability and Collaboration*, 53
Human–Computer Interaction Series, DOI 10.1007/978-1-4471-5499-0_5,
© Springer-Verlag London 2013

Fig. 5.1 A group of four students performing a Web search with TwisterSearch. Each student was assigned to a *red*, *green*, *yellow*, or *blue* color with which to identify themselves during the search process. The Apple iPad allows solitary Web searches as well as a seamless transition between different coupling styles without hindering others

when assisting users in the three search phases identified by Evans and Chi in their canonical model of social search based on everyday searches, including before search, during search, and after search [9].

While most present-day systems for collaborative Web searches focus on the during search phase, they lack support for other phases that are more collaborative and they are often distributed in nature and require a division of labor. For example, a survey conducted by Morris showed that 22.0 % of the respondents cooperated by brainstorming or suggesting keywords to each other for generation and refinement purposes before the search [7] – a process that is currently unsupported.

Furthermore, we believe that DUIs based on post-desktop computing systems such as tabletops and tablets are important for a natural collaboration and for supporting different working styles. For example, Jetter et al. provide collaborative faceted search and flexible working styles using a hybrid visual-tangible user interface on a tabletop that users perceived as fun to use and that was equally effective as traditional Web interfaces [4].

Our goal is to achieve a similar result for collaborative Web searches based on a Samsung SUR40 with Microsoft® PixelSense™ tabletop and Apple iPad tablets. In the following, we first propose design goals for systems supporting collaborative Web searches based on the canonical model of social search by Evans and Chi [9] and implications for design of Morris [7]. Then, we present TwisterSearch[1] (Fig. 5.1), an interactive prototype that we designed and

---

[1]TwisterSearch Video – http://hci.uni-konstanz.de/researchprojects/twistersearch

implemented to meet these design goals, and describe its interaction design using a scenario. Thereafter, a real-life study demonstrates its overall usability for educational purposes. We conclude with a brief summary and our plans for future work.

5.2   Design Goals

We have formulated four design goals (DG1-4) based on the canonical model of social search by Evans and Chi [9] and design indications given by Morris [7]: *(1). Support Strategic Planning and Coordination, (2). Amplify Collaboration, (3). Intensify Discussion and Simplify User Input,* and *(4). Facility Traceability of Evidence Files.* We consider all four of the DGs to be critical for the successful design of a post-WIMP DUI for collaborative Web searches. Therefore, our prototype TwisterSearch was designed and implemented with regard to these DGs.

5.2.1   DG1: Support Strategic Planning and Coordination

Morris describes two search strategies that occur in cooperative search tasks: divide-and-conquer and brute force [7]. The first is a coordinated division of labor whereas the latter is uncoordinated and tends to evoke "Google races" or "competitions." These races could duplicate search results and thus increase search effort. Therefore, we argue that providing tool support for explicit coordination and planning of an on-going search leads towards a structured search. Users should be supported in pre-search activities (e.g., framing contexts and refining requirements) and post-search activities (e.g., organizing and distributing search results). Thereby, framing the context defines and clarifies the boundaries of an intended future search task and establishes informational needs and motives among the group members. Refining the search requirements solidifies informational needs in a step-by-step manner by consulting other sources, such as colleagues. Later, structuring and distribution of search results takes place in 72.0 % of the reported search experiences and is a pre-condition for embedding searches into real world activities and decision making [9].

5.2.2   DG2: Amplify Collaboration

Evans and Chi categorized the during search phase into three different behaviors: navigational, transactional, and informational search [9]. Based on their survey, the latter accounts for more than half (59.3 %) of the search intentions and includes various steps, from information foraging to sense-making. The informational search behavior, furthermore, features both solitary tasks (e.g., reading and extracting information) as well as informational exchange with others. A Web search system, therefore, should best offer a smooth transition between loosely-coupled parallel work and tightly-coupled collaboration similar to [3, 4].

5.2.3   DG3: Intensify Discussion and Simplify User Input

Conventional WIMP interfaces with their single point-of-action are inappropriate for creating shareable user interfaces for co-located collaborative work. In these cases, simultaneous user input is indispensable. In contrast, Geyer et al. show the feasibility of a post-WIMP tabletop and tangible user interface combined with digital pen and paper for creative group work [10]. Furthermore, touch interfaces, such as tabletops, allow users to communicate more efficiently with the help of deictic references to create a joint reference and substantiate arguments. Although touch input is the dominant input on tabletops, a study conducted by Morris et al. also discovered issues when using virtual keyboards on tabletops for search term input and propose the integration of physical keyboards instead [5]. We further believe that collaborative Web search systems enable verbal and non-verbal face-to-face communication and more natural gesturing to intensify discussion and to yield superior outcomes. Besides these effects on communication, a simplified user input also allows users to focus on the primary search task instead of being busy with secondary tasks, such as text input.

5.2.4   DG4: Facilitate Traceability of Evidence Files

Gathering results and additional information automatically during a search allows users to trace the directions of the search and the keywords used to find the results. Morris [7] writes that "this information helps collaborators understand what techniques have already been tried and how to interpret the authoritativeness or appropriateness of the results." Thus, we consider traceability to be an important aspect, especially if Web searches are carried out over several sessions.

5.3   System Design

Based on the four design goals, we designed and implemented our prototype TwisterSearch. TwisterSearch is a distributed user interface running on a shared display and multiple private displays. The shared display is used to collaboratively collect search results in a visual workspace. This workspace is provided on a Samsung SUR40 with Microsoft® PixelSense™ tabletop providing multi-touch input and additionally recognizes physical objects placed on the surface (tokens).

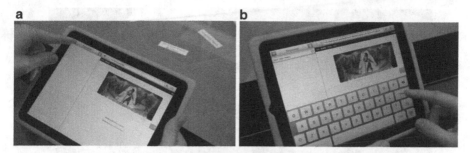

Fig. 5.2 Add new keywords to the search. (**a**) Tap on the '+' sign on the *top left*. (**b**) A keyboard appears and you can enter the keyword. Press the 'Done' button on the keyboard to confirm the keyword, which sends it to the shared space automatically

Private pad-sized displays (Apple iPads) are used around the table to individually search the Web and share findings with co-workers on the shared display. The following short scenario provides an example for a typical usage situation.

At the beginning of a history course, four students are requested to do research about the history of Switzerland. They are asked to collect facts about its culture, topology, and politics and write an essay about their findings by the end of the term. They are allowed to do this as a group. The group meets at the library where a workroom is equipped with TwisterSearch. The four students sit around the tabletop and each user takes a TwisterSearch set consisting of an Apple iPad and a small tablet token (see Fig. 5.1). This token is a small acrylic and tablet-shaped glass block with a colored frame. Each set and thus each user has a unique color (red, green, blue, yellow) that is also visible as the color of the iPad's cover and the frame of the tablet token. Before the group members start their individual search activities, they connect their private displays to the shared space by starting the TwisterSearch app on the iPad. A user halo (colored oval) appears at edge of the shared display and indicates that the connection is functioning properly (see Fig. 5.1). Next, they start to frame the topic (DG1). For this purpose, all users type in relevant keywords on their iPads using the virtual keyboard and send the keywords to the shared space by pressing the 'Done' button (see Fig. 5.2) (DG3). Then, keywords are displayed instantly on the shared space in the user's color and close to the user's halo.

Collecting keywords is either done in parallel or as a joint effort in which team members recommend keywords or consult other group members for relevant terms (DG2, DG3). This process leads to a framing of the search's context and results in a collaborative construction of a skeleton of keywords, which is filled with search results in the next step. The keywords appear in the four colors that are each assigned to a single user, which provides a great degree of traceability (DG4). It is possible for one user to start clustering keywords according to their semantic coherence while the others are collecting additional keywords. However, clustering can also be done as a joint effort supported by discussion (DG3).

Clusters are created and become visible when a user encircles one or more keywords using his or her finger. Furthermore, clusters can overlap to convey the search topic (e.g., Switzerland) (Fig. 5.3). Since requirements are often refined in

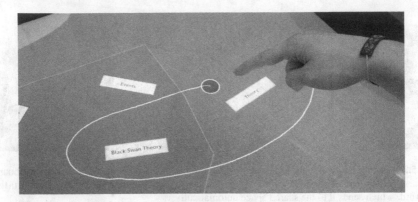

Fig. 5.3 Touch input is used to cluster keywords and to frame the context of the intended informational search

Fig. 5.4 You can lift a keyword by touching and dragging it on the screen. A successful lift will be indicated using a drop shadow effect and a matrix transform

social searches, users can change existing clusters and cluster content at any time. For instance, they can add new keywords, rearrange keywords to different clusters, or split clusters. To lift a keyword virtually, simply has to touch and release it as desired. Lifting and dropping is animated using a drop shadow effect and a matrix transform, which surrogates a behavior similar to moving a real scrap of paper (Fig. 5.4). Moreover, keywords can be removed and put inside the user halo for later usage. After students agree on clustering, the group members are assigned to different clusters by putting the users' corresponding tablet tokens on different clusters (DG1). The token indicates who is responsible for which search so that collaborators know who is searching for information for a specific cluster. This highly increases the group's overall awareness of what each member is doing. Moreover, you can transfer cluster keywords to the linked Apple iPad by placing a token on a cluster.

Now, individual searches are performed on private displays. This can be done either loosely coupled in parallel (no 'backseat driving' [7]) or tightly-coupled in

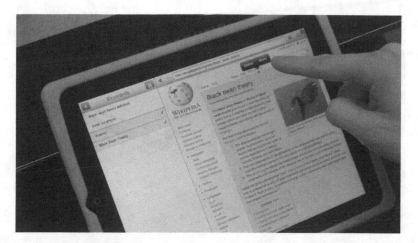

Fig. 5.5 The TwisterSearch user interface on an Apple iPad featuring keywords of a selected cluster (*left column*) and a Web browser (*right column*)

collaboration (DG2), such as when showing interesting websites to co-workers. Moreover, novice searchers can learn vocabulary and syntax from experts when searching in close collaboration [7] and apply their knowledge instantly. On the private display, received keywords are displayed in the left column and a Web browser is displayed in the right column (Fig. 5.5). A user selects one or more keywords by tapping on them. Then, a 'Google' search is initiated automatically using the selected keywords and consequently displays 'Google' search results. Users can browse through provided links or adjust the search manually. The browser is operated as known from the Apple iPad Safari app. A complete website or parts of it can be selected by touching and holding the information until the selection rectangle shows up. A 'Share' button then appears above or below the selection. By pressing the 'Share' button, the selected information, including search paths taken and user ID, is transferred to the shared display. The result is displayed immediately in the result view of the cluster on the shared display (Fig. 5.6). Each cluster has its own scrollable result view. Users can hand over private displays to show and exchange interesting information before sharing them with the group. All results can be reviewed on the shared display and private displays at any time. Tapping a result on the shared display opens the corresponding result on all private displays linked through tablet tokens, which is useful for discussion and especially important when defining arguments for the final outcome (DG3).

After a Web search session, results can be automatically stored on any kind of removable disk by connecting it via USB to the Samsung SUR40. The TwisterSearch application creates a dedicated folder on that disk and saves images and Web sites to that folder. This allows the group to distribute or organize results from a collaborative Web search session (DG4).

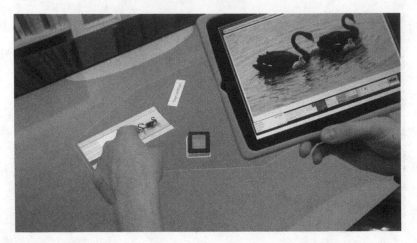

Fig. 5.6 Tapping a result in the result view on the shared display opens the same result in more detail on the private display

5.4 Implementation

The application on the shared display (server) is implemented in C#/WPF with the .NET 4.0 framework and the application on the private display (client) is implemented in iOS 5. The cluster visualization on the Samsung SUR40 displays a convex hull to indicate encircled objects. A Windows Communication Foundation (WCF) Web service and OSC[2] is used for client/server communication. The shared display renders Web content with help of Awesomium.[3] The clients communicate with the server via WCF Web service, which will be opened on the Samsung SUR40 on application startup. Multicast OSC messages distribute keywords and the object IDs of existing results to the clients. Theoretically, the implementation of TwisterSearch supports unlimited clients; however, the table size constrains the number of collaborators to a maximum of four. BaseX[4] persists session data, all results including search paths and the user ID, all connection data, and the interaction log. The latter will be used to evaluate the system in a controlled experiment.

5.5 Evaluation

We conducted a formative study to find out if TwisterSearch is capable of meeting our assumed design goals for collaborative Web searches and if it mediates during pre-, during-, and post-search activities. This includes general and situated

---

[2] Open Sound Control (OSC) – http://opensoundcontrol.org/

[3] Awesomium is a web-ui bridge for native apps – http://awesomium.com/

[4] BaseX is a light-weight XML database – http://basex.org

Fig. 5.7 Participants of the study searching the Web for evidence files. Each participant is wearing two bracelets (*right* and *left wrist*) according to their assigned TwisterSearch color. In this group, 2×2 participants had to share an iPad since the group consisted of six people and the prototype is equipped with four private displays only. The bracelets of the sharing partners have the same color but can be distinguished as one has plain colored bracelets and the other has colored bracelets with black stripes

awareness of the actions of co-workers and the applicability of TwisterSearch to the canonical model of social searches. Moreover, we wanted to identify barriers, "where the user must stop and learn many new concepts and techniques to make further progress" [11]. Therefore, we tested TwisterSearch in an educational setting and conducted the study in a high school with five groups in five different school subjects. Each subject was taught by a different teacher. We provided the teachers with one Samsung SUR40, four iPads, and both TwisterSearch applications for the table as well as for the iPads. The only requirement given to the teachers was that they had to prepare a lesson that demanded group work.

The tasks originate from the regular curriculum and were defined by the teachers themselves. Moreover, the teachers were not introduced to the technology beforehand; thus, the contents of teaching were made independently to allow us to test the general applicability of TwisterSearch to different teaching styles. Also, we did not want to purport assignment of tasks and thus avoid artificial tasks in advance.

The study generated data from pre- and post-test questionnaires (demographical, technical background), video recordings, interviews, and observations. During the study, the participants had to wear bracelets according to their assigned TwisterSearch color to distinguish the participants in the later video analysis (Fig. 5.7). The participants were asked to think aloud if they faced any problems or if they thought an important function was missing.

Fig. 5.8 The computer room with classmates performing the same task in groups of the same size. The *door in the back* connects to the observation room

A group consisted of 4–6 students, which result in an overall count of 23 students (20 male, 3 female). The mean age is 17.7 years (SD = 1.07, min = 16, max = 20). Their mean computer experience in years is 9.65 (SD = 1.95, min = 7, max = 14) and all participants had prior experience with touch-sensitive displays (e.g. smartphone, ATM, ticket machine, etc.). The mean value of their self-assessment of computer affinity is 3.04 (SD = 0.69, min = 2), ranging from 1 = beginner to 5 = expert. The daily usage of computers is M = 2.0 (SD = 0.88) whereas the scale is 1 = '$\leq$ 1 h', 2 = '1 to $\leq$ 2 h', 3 = '2 to $\leq$ 3 h', and 4 = '> 3 h.'

The school subjects included in the study were Business Studies, Global Studies, Financial Management, German, and Geography. One group of each class was selected to perform their task with TwisterSearch while the other students had to use conventional desktop computers as illustrated in Fig. 5.8.

During the tasks, the test supervisor was present simply to provide assistance if technical issues occurred or usability issues hindered students in continuing their work since the study was meant to simulate an in "real life" setting. The teachers, however, were still allowed to help whenever task related questions arose.

Each group had a double period (90 min) to fulfill the given task, excluding time for technical instruction regarding the system as well as the training phase. Each function of the prototype was explained at first without pointing the students to the specific procedure that was derived from the canonical model of social searches. Afterwards, the students had enough time to "play" with TwisterSearch before doing the task and until they felt confident enough to operate the system.

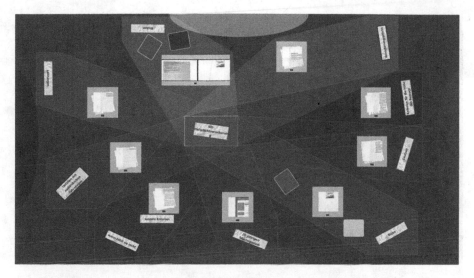

Fig. 5.9 The group followed the intrinsic procedure implemented in TwisterSearch, which is based on the canonical model of social searches

5.6 Results

The final outcomes of groups' Web search sessions differ in several aspects. Of course, the outcome depends on the task but also on the strategy a group chose to solve the task. In the following, we picked three final outcomes of Web search sessions to present two working styles that occurred most frequently during the study and one case were TwisterSearch was used for purposes other than originally intended (Figs. 5.9, 5.10, and 5.11).

Although, none of the groups were forced to follow the intended process of TwisterSearch, this group immediately started by brainstorming and collected keywords they thought of to be relevant to fulfill the task. Their task was to search for different qualities of vehicle insurance and provide a basic set of dimensions to qualitatively compare these insurance policies (e.g., compulsory insurance or liability in the event of damage). They generated the main topic 'vehicle insurance' in the center and started to diffuse in eight dimensions (clusters, see Fig. 5.9). After all members agreed on the skeleton of keywords, the group assigned the individual dimensions to single group members. Their approach confirms to the pre-search activity and DG1 and therefore avoids 'Google races.' The Web search was performed solitary by the individual group members. After a group member was satisfied with the results, that person's responsibility changed to the next cluster. At the end of the search, participants put all tablet tokens into a single cluster and the person responsible for that cluster explained the contents. Other group members placed comprehensive questions, if necessary. However, the group did not

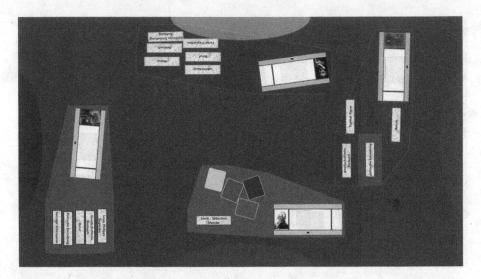

Fig. 5.10 A final outcome without prior brainstorming

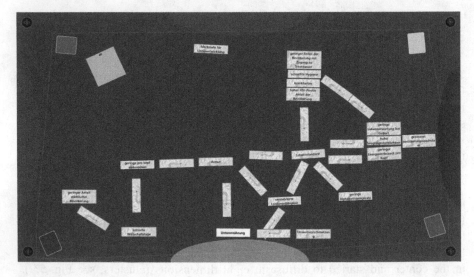

Fig. 5.11 The final outcome of a group that used TwisterSearch as a mind mapping tool

discuss or argue for or against certain results. The study did not clarify whether all participants were simply satisfied with the results or if TwisterSearch provides insufficient support for such discussion (DG3).

Another group started without brainstorming. Their task was to create a fact file for famous personalities (e.g., Louis Philippe Legendre or Thomas Paine). Beforehand, the teacher assigned each student with a known personality and instructed them to explain and discuss the facts once they were finished with their search. This led to four unique clusters in which each participant collected keywords individually (Fig. 5.10). However, the group exchanged valuable Web sources through face-to-face communication during the search. Again, this group did not discuss the results despite the fact that they explained the facts they found to other group members after the search. This resembles previous observations. Future studies should address this in more detail.

The third outcome illustrated in Fig. 5.11 is noteworthy since this group did not collect any Web resources. Instead they used TwisterSearch as a mind map tool to visualize the impact factors of standards of living. Of course, TwisterSearch was not implemented to be used as a mind mapping tool initially because of the missing functionality needed to create links between keywords. The group, however, managed to link words by creating keywords with ASCII-links (e.g., uni-directional links like "———>"). The private devices were only used to create keywords and to obtain keywords by searching on task-related Web sites.

All participants were instructed to report on any problem and missing features during the study, which was jotted down by the investigator. For instance, two groups wanted to send links to websites without sharing them as a result. They requested it in order to start searching from the same informational base (other than 'Google'). The participants bypassed this by directing their team members to the website manually. Likewise, participants wanted to send selected text as keyword from the browser to the shared space instead of typing it manually. At the current stage of the prototype, it is impossible to alter the keyword text. The participants had to delete the keyword first and add a keyword with the corrected text thereafter. One group asked to be able to drag and drop the results from the result view on the landscape to freely arrange result items in clusters. Groups with a good number of keywords had an often cluttered landscape and several attempts by different participants were made to move entire clusters together with all keyword. Such requests to pan the landscape could imply the future integration of a zoomable user interface (ZUI) like ZOIL [12].

The qualitative feedback obtained through interviews indicates a better received quality of group work when asked for differences between regular group work and group work mediated by TwisterSearch. For instance, a participant mentioned that "Everyone can contribute to the work in an equal manner," which confirms DG2. Moreover, all participants reported having better awareness of the current and ongoing situation both for search responsibilities as well as completeness of the overall task. For instance, one participant argued that, "It is immediately apparent what the others are doing." However, the participant also criticized the longer period of vocational adjustment.

In addition to the study, we demonstrated TwisterSearch to teachers who were not taking part at the current study. These teachers were attracted by the didactic opportunities such a technology can provide. One teacher even mentioned a didactic method called Metaplan,[5] which follows similar principles as those that

---

[5] http://en.wikipedia.org/wiki/Metaplan

TwisterSearch incorporates. First, Metaplan requires a brainstorming phase where participants (a group of students) collect keywords on index cards and pin them on cork board. Of course, the collected keywords must match to the given task and are continuously clustered and augmented with strokes and arrows to express a common visual mind map. In some cases, teachers take a digital picture of the cork board and hand it out to students or students have to write down the mind map manually. With this as a basis, the group starts searching the Web for relevant information and assigns them directly to keywords on the visual mind map. The result of such a Metaplan session could be a poster or presentation.

This is very interesting for our research, as well-known didactic practices can be used in school subjects without necessarily changing the methodology to incorporate computer assistance.

The students in the computer room as illustrated in Fig. 5.8 are equipped with one personal computer each and groups were either seated in rows or blocks of 2x2 (two computers in a row and two rows). They were allowed to use tools of their choice to solve the task (e.g., Internet Explorer, etc.) and although exchange drives are provided by the school, most students used Facebook as platform in which to share teaching materials with their group members. This social platform allowed students to communicate with each other without yelling at each other in the classroom. However, they had to leave their workplace if face-to-face communication was required to show and highlight important aspects on a website.

5.7 Conclusion and Future Work

Based on the canonical model of social search by Evans and Chi [9] and implications for design described by Morris [7], we identified four design goals for the emerging topic of DUIs for collaborative search: *(1). Support Strategic Planning and Coordination, (2). Amplify Collaboration, (3). Intensify Discussion and Simplify User Input, and (4). Facilitate Traceability of Evidence Files*. On this basis, we presented the design and implementation of our interactive prototype TwisterSearch, which uses post-WIMP interaction with a tabletop computers and tablets to distribute collaborative Web searches across device boundaries. In a next step, we evaluated to what extent our design meets the design goals and enables efficient collaborative Web searches for educational purposes. Therefore, we conducted a qualitative user study similar to WeSearch [5]. After this, we will make TwisterSearch accessible to a broader user population in the library of the University of Konstanz to recruit participants for a controlled experiment with real library users and students in our lab.

Acknowledgments This work was partially supported by DFG Research Training Group GK-1042 "Explorative Analysis and Visualization of Large Information Spaces," University of Konstanz, and by the Ministry for Science, Research, and Art Baden-Wurttemberg under the project Blended Library.[6] We especially thank Thomas Rädle and his colleagues at LES Sigmaringen for providing us the opportunity to evaluate and embed TwisterSearch in current classes, which served as an "real life" setting far beyond what controlled experiments and laboratories could offer.

References

1. Amershi, S., & Morris, M. R. (2008). CoSearch: A system for co-located collaborative web search. *Proceedings of the Twenty-Sixth Annual Sigchi Conference on Human Factors in Computing Systems – Proc. CHI 2008* (pp. 1647–1656).
2. Heilig, M. et al. (2011). Hidden details of negotiation: The mechanics of reality-based collaboration in information seeking. *Proceedings of the 13th IFIP TC 13 International Conference on Human-Computer Interaction – Volume Part II (INTERACT'11)* (pp. 622–639). Springer-Verlag, Berlin/Heidelberg.
3. Isenberg, P., & Fisher, D. (2009). Collaborative brushing and linking for co-located visual analytics of document collections. *Computer Graphics Forum, 28*(3), 1031–1038.
4. Jetter, H. C. et al. (2011). Materializing the query with facet-streams – A hybrid surface for collaborative search on tabletops. *Proceedings of the 2011 Annual Conference on Human Factors in Computing Systems (CHI'11)* (pp. 3013–3022). ACM, New York.
5. Morris, M. R. et al. (2010). WeSearch: Supporting collaborative search and sensemaking on a tabletop display. *Proceedings of the 2010 ACM Conference on Computer Supported Cooperative Work – CSCW'10* (pp. 401–410). New York: ACM Press.
6. Paul, S., & Morris, M. (2009). CoSense: Enhancing sensemaking for collaborative web search. *Proceedings of the SIGCHI Conference on Human Factors in Computing Systems (CHI'09)* (pp. 1771). ACM Press, New York.
7. Morris, M. R. (2008). A survey of collaborative web search practices. *Proceeding of the Twenty-Sixth Annual CHI Conference on Human Factors in Computing Systems – CHI'08.* 1657.
8. Elmqvist, N. (2011). Distributed user interfaces: State of the art. In J. A. Gallud et al. (Eds.), *Distributed user interfaces: Designing interfaces for the distributed ecosystem* (pp. 1–12). London: Springer.
9. Evans, B. M., & Chi, E. H. (2010). An elaborated model of social search. *Information Processing & Management, 46*(6), 656–678.
10. Geyer, F. et al. (2011). Designing reality-based interfaces for creative group work. *Proceedings of the 8th ACM Conference on Creativity and Cognition – C&C'11* (p. 165). ACM Press, New York.
11. Myers, B., et al. (2000). Past, present, and future of user interface software tools. *ACM Transactions on Computer-Human Interaction (TOCHI), 7*(1), 3–28.
12. Zöllner, M., et al. (2011). ZOIL: A design paradigm and software framework for post-WIMP distributed user inter-faces. In J. A. Gallud et al. (Eds.), *Distributed user interfaces: Designing interfaces for the distributed ecosystem* (pp. 87–94). London: Springer.

---

[6]http://hci.uni-konstanz.de/blendedlibrary/

Chapter 6
Integration of Collaborative Features in Ubiquitous and Context-Aware Systems Using Distributed User Interfaces

Juan E. Garrido, Víctor M.R. Penichet, and María D. Lozano

Abstract Collaboration is essential in healthcare environments for a wide variety of tasks and situations. Health practitioners have to perform complex tasks, which in turn are divided in more simple ones and workers can assist each other when doubts or unexpected situations occur. In the latter case, if the situation is an emergency, it needs to be solved first and then, pending tasks are again reorganized within their well-defined agenda. These changing conditions, which might result in an adaptation of the employees' behavior, create the need of ubiquitous and context-aware software that offers information and functionality based on their needs. Additionally, many healthcare employees need to use the same application through different devices depending on their context, as they are constantly moving around the environment. The system should adapt its display window based on the device restrictions through a distributed user interface. In this paper, we present Ubi4health as a system whose main features include the aforementioned healthcare requirements. The system presents, as a differential factor in healthcare settings, the use of the distributed user interface paradigm within ubiquitous environments, which favours the collaborative work. Finally, we present the outcomes of the usability evaluation performed on the system based on the ISO 9126–4.

J.E. Garrido (✉)
Computer Science Research Institute, University of Castilla-La Mancha, Albacete, Spain
e-mail: juanenrique.garrido@uclm.es

V.M.R. Penichet • M.D. Lozano
Computing Systems Department, University of Castilla-La Mancha, Albacete, Spain
e-mail: victor.penichet@uclm.es; maria.lozano@uclm.es

M.D. Lozano et al. (eds.), *Distributed User Interfaces: Usability and Collaboration*,
Human–Computer Interaction Series, DOI 10.1007/978-1-4471-5499-0_6,
© Springer-Verlag London 2013

6.1   Introduction

Healthcare environments [1–4] have always been an objective when applying new technologies. An expected consequence is to make easier the performance of employees' tasks. Physicians, as healthcare employees, continuously face complex and delicate task conditions. They have to adapt their task in process to changes that happen constantly in their work environment. For example, in a hospital, while a nurse is measuring blood pressure, an emergency comes up and a workmate calls him for help. Therefore, s/he has to stop his activity at that moment and carry on again later, which implies reorganizing his agenda in a dynamic way. New technologies can help support those changes and offer medical staff an adequate way to manage their daily work.

Often physicians need to move around in their work center. They have to visit many patients and perform different tasks in different locations. When nurses are treating a patient and they need information about his medical record, they have to go to the place where it is kept. It implies a waste of time, an essential feature in healthcare. Therefore, healthcare systems should be ubiquitous [5–8] in order to allow employees to use them wherever and whenever they are required. In addition, collaboration [9–13] and context-awareness [14–18] are two features which may accompany ubiquity in healthcare due to the capabilities they provide.

Many tasks require collaboration from two or more health workers. For example, in order to examine a patient's blood test, a doctor and a nurse have to collaborate. First, the nurse has to extract the blood and send it to the laboratory. Then, the doctor will read and study the results of the blood test. In healthcare, collaborative tasks can imply coordination, as several dependent steps may be involved. It could also be possible that they are so complicated that more than one person is required to perform the said task. Therefore, users of healthcare systems should be capable of collaborating with others if so required.

Context-awareness is a key feature in healthcare systems. The medical staff needs to be aware [19] of what is happening around them [16]. They need to know who is available at an specific moment and what resources are available, which tasks are in process, who is using something, etc. Hence, a context-aware system will be very useful in healthcare environments; healthcare employees can be more efficient if they have in their devices the information they need according to their current state, situation and task. A good example is when a doctor is going to apply a daily treatment to his current patient. He needs to know the availability and localization of the medicines and the medical tools he has to use. This is information that a healthcare system may show to the doctor automatically depending on his context.

Ubi4health -the system we present in this paper- provides different mechanisms to improve collaborative work in this type of settings. The association of collaboration, ubiquity and context-awareness in the same system offers employees the possibility of collaborating with their workmates, providing the information and the functionality they need (based on their context) anytime and anywhere. Collaboration can be enhanced if the employees can work with their devices using distributed user interfaces. This capacity allows users to work around the environment regardless of the device they use at any moment due to the distribution of the application in different devices. The main contribution of this approach is not just a healthcare application (there are many of this kind, as discussed later), but a combination of key concepts such as collaboration, ubiquity and context-awareness, all together, in order to improve task performance in a healthcare center. Such an application provides collaborative features as well as an emergency system which coordinates them if needed. Additionally, employees can use different devices depending on their context: they could use a personal computer if they do not need to move; or they can use a PDA, a smartphone or a mobile device, if they need to complete their task moving in the environment. Anyhow, the system offers users the same application with different display windows. We have selected a real residential care home as the perfect environment to implement the system thanks to the collaboration requirements of its staff. However, Ubi4health can be used in most of healthcare environments.

The rest of the paper is organized as follows: a description of outstanding related works is presented in Sect. 6.2. Section 6.3 describes the system focused on its architecture, main functionality and its contributions through a comparison of related works. The outcomes of Ubi4health's evaluation are described in Sect. 6.4. Finally, Sect. 6.5 presents conclusions and future work.

6.2 Related Works

Over the last decade, healthcare has appeared as a relevant research field and many research groups have focused their interests on it. One of the main reasons for this fact is the capacity to improve the tasks required in healthcare environments, such as hospitals, residential care homes, clinics, etc. In this way, several systems and prototypes have been developed in order to facilitate the realization of essential processes in medical environments. Following, outstanding related works with Ubi4health are described. The study of these systems allows to make comparisons and to indicate which is our contribution in the field of ubiquitous healthcare.

MobileWARD [20] is the oldest remarkable related work. The system is a context-aware electronic patient record designed in agreement with two ideas: (a) to analyze the user's context and react according to it; (b) and to provide a correct interaction process through his fingers. MobileWARD detects the entrance of a user in a ward and automatically displays the information related to the ward. For example, the system displays the exact location of users and patients in that ward.

Awaremedia and Awarephone [21] are two context-aware applications oriented to hospitals which use Bluetooth technology to locate employees. More specifically, the applications use a modified Bluetooth USB whose range of action is diminished due to some modifications. Awaremedia is an application developed for interactive devices. It includes icons representing each user: his image, localization, state and diary. Awarephone is an application developed for phones with Symbian. It shows information about the tasks and location of workmates. Additionally, the system offers a communication channel for users through a messages chat.

Another related work focused in location information is a specific tracking system for disoriented patients [22]. The authors intend to show the acceptance of ubiquitous devices in healthcare. More specifically, they create a WLAN infrastructure with which they are able to locate disoriented patients. The infrastructure consists in a big amount of Cisco WLAN Access points (170) located around the environment, a residential care home. The system is completed by providing patients (attached into their clothes) with an AeroScout Tag, a WLAN component, which was specially developed to locate people or special medical devices. Each tag communicates with the WLAN infrastructure in programmable and intermittent temporal intervals. The staff assigns one tag to each patient, so the system can control the patient's movements automatically sending alarms when the patient leaves a specific area.

The closest related work to Ubi4health is iHospital [23]. iHospital is a smart environment to assist hospital staff activities by trying to comply with the main requirements of a healthcare environment: high mobility, constant activity switching, the need to coordinate activities with workmates and the abundance of information. The system is an ideal representation of a highly interactive workplace, where the healthcare staff can access relevant medical information through a set of heterogeneous devices and collaborate, taking into account their own context. iHospital is ubiquitous and context-aware, so (1) users can access needed information anytime and anywhere; and (2) the system offers a context-aware communication system, which means that devices are used to monitor and derive relevant contextual information, such as the location of people and artifacts that users may need to complete their tasks. These are two key features as they will reduce an important gap in healthcare environments: the task time. Some other important features of iHospital are the following: supporting the mobile Hospital Electronic Medical Record, providing hospital tools to back mobile Clinical Decision Making, boosting the nature of multitasking and integrating the physical and digital domain.

The last two remarkable related works are an assistant task manager for physicians [24] and VERA [25]. The first one includes a bracelet (for each user) whose behavior is programmed by the assistant. The bracelet warns with colors explicit alerts. For example, if a serum bottle must be changed, a red light will switch on. In turn, VERA is a phone-based system that increases awareness about health behavior taking medical decisions. The user, through an Android application, takes a photo and follows the following steps: (1) identify the behavior related to the photo; (2) selects or proposes the appropriate procedure, and (3) write comments. In this way, users with group condition can see other photos, analyze their behavior and then, take the correct decision.

The vast majority of the related works abovementioned did not consider the possibility of integrating ubiquitous, context-aware and collaborative features in the same system. Ubi4health combines these features to allow healthcare employees to work with a collaborative tool that manages dynamically the tasks to be done and creates automatic reminders. The system is responsible for assigning tasks in a context-sensitive way and make sure that all tasks are done. In addition, Ubi4health warns in the most adequate employees when an emergency comes up. The system detects the nearest employees available and sends them a request. Regarding complexity, Ubi4health uses common devices (personal computers, laptops, PDAs or mobile devices) and simple WLAN infrastructure. This is an improvement as compared to other previous related works that usually need complex infrastructures or devices to create ubiquitous and context-aware environments. However, this comparison between Ubi4health and related works will be completed in Sect. 6.3 emphasizing its main contributions.

6.3   Ubi4health System

In healthcare environments, each shift includes numerous tasks related to resident or patient care which have to be done by the appropriate health worker. The implications of healthcare tasks entail a management style different from that in other work centers or environments. The main implication is patient care, a powerful reason to consider healthcare task management as special.

Ubi4health is a system designed to improve the performance of daily duties in a residential care home, but it could be also applied in other medical centers. It is ubiquitous, context-aware and collaborative, characteristics which create an adequate environment to successfully complete residential care home tasks. Users will have any information required anywhere and anytime based on their context (location, current tasks, needed resources, etc.) being able to receive assistance by workmates.

Ubiquity offers a hidden system to employees in their daily workplace. They will have the capacity to access any information or functionality at any moment and place. Users do not need to know how the system works, they only have to use the client application to perform their tasks wherever they are.

Context-awareness is an essential feature in our system. Ubi4health offers the information and functionality that users need based on their current task and location. That means, users will have automatically in their client application, whatever they need based on where they are, what task they are performing, what resources they need, who are near and are able to help, etc. In this sense, we have studied previously a real residential care home in order to know the employees' requirements related to information and functionality in order to perform their tasks.

Collaboration is the third important feature to be considered in Ubi4health. In a residential care home, employees often need to be assisted to complete their tasks in many situations. Some tasks are collaborative by nature; for example, when a resident has to be cleaned and he can't move his legs. In this case, almost two employees may collaborate to complete that task. In other cases, the evolution of a task can involve that a user requires help. For example, when a nurse who is

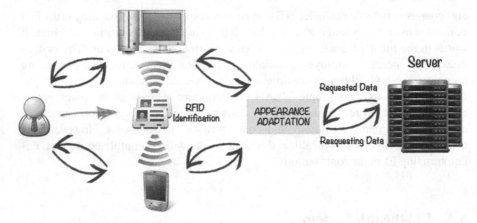

Fig. 6.1 System architecture

measuring the blood pressure of a resident and suddenly, the resident falls down to the floor because of dizziness. In that situation, the nurse needs someone to move the resident to the medical area.

The next subsections explain the architecture needed to deploy Ubi4health and how it works in order to facilitate the daily work of the employees in a residential care home.

6.3.1 Technology and Architecture

The system architecture has been divided into two sub-architectures: software and hardware. The software architecture follows a client–server model and it consists of mobile and desktop applications (the client part) and the server application where the information will be managed.

The mobile application has been designed in order to be deployed in mobile devices or PDAs with Windows Mobile 5.0 or next versions. The devices must incorporate wireless connection based on 802.11 standards and an RFID reader to allow the identification of employees.

The server has two main components. The first component is the database that stores any data related to employees, residents, alerts, tasks, etc. The second component is a web service collection with capacity to perform any database action in order to manage information needed by client applications.

The hardware architecture (see Fig. 6.1) has been obtained by studying the infrastructure that the software components needs. In this way, the system offers desktop PCs or laptops to the users who do not need mobility around the environment; and PDAs to the users who will be moving in any place of the center. Also, each user will have an identification card with an RFID tag to facilitate the identification task which is done through RFID readers incorporated to each PDA.

The communication is supported through a set of WIFI access points located around the residential care home to offer connection at any location in the center. We use a WIFI infrastructure to locate healthcare staff in the environment. The process consists of detecting each mobile device, near wireless signals. The strongest signal determines where the device is, because it corresponds to the WIFI access point located in the same zone where the device is connected. The environment has been divided into different zones, each one associated to a specific access point. Therefore, the system can establish where a user is depending on the access connection point. The healthcare center may consist of more than one floor, so the strongest Wi-Fi signal can belong to an access point located in other floor. Consequently, the location infrastructure includes RFID readers placed at each point of the center in all floors. When a user location changes to other floor, the system detects the change by reading the identity RFID card. In this way, the system does not consider access points which are in different floors from the location of the target employee.

An important aspect is that it is not necessary to know exactly the point in the environment where a user is because the zones have been established and organized according to it. Each zone has a maximum distance so if a workmate has to cover it to attend an emergency, it will not be a problem.

6.3.2 Description of the System

Ubi4health has been developed as a prototype whose main axe is the healthcare staff. The system will be centered in the functions and tasks that healthcare employees might attend in their daily work. Moreover, Ubi4health functionality is described stressing the contribution in healthcare, with the objective to avoid being seen as a simple tutorial. The system is designed to reach the following objectives through several devices (Personal Computers, Laptops, PDAs and Mobile Phones), thus providing complete mobility:

- *Managing tasks to be performed by healthcare staff.* Since there are many tasks to accomplish in a residential care home, the system provides a list of tasks to be assigned along the time based on active users and available resources. In this case, if a user is doing a task with a low urgency level and his location is adequate to do any unassigned task, the system will warn the user and the user will be automatically assigned to such a task. Therefore, the system offers a simple but effective method to automatically assign pending tasks.

  Additionally, employees can manage their own tasks through the application. The application gives users the possibility to access their personal agenda, where they can see when each assigned task is planned to start and a detailed description. An example of a user agenda is shown in Fig. 6.2. Additionally, the agenda allows users to mark each task as "done" or if they are allowed, mark it as "unassigned". They also may create (see Fig. 6.2) their own notes. This possibility is fundamental because it allows users to create auxiliary tasks to be

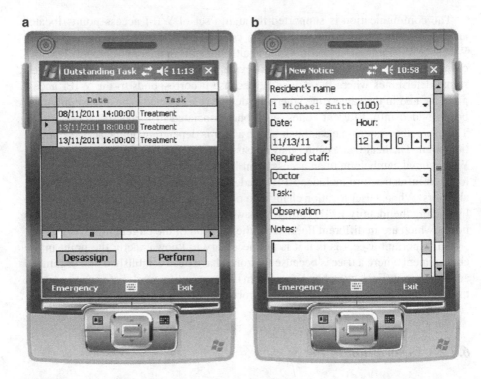

Fig. 6.2 Employee task to be done (**a**) and advice creation (**b**)

done in a different shift, thus avoiding forgetting oral indications or comments between employees. For example, if a nurse checks during a routine task that a resident has abnormal blood pressure, they can indicate with a note that the pressure should be measured again in two hours.

- *Improving communication between employees using a note synchronous system.* The mechanism operates like an email system, creating a note for a workmate who will receive it immediately. The idea is to eliminate the action of walking to look for a workmate in the workplace to ask or tell something, thus preventing time waste. This communication mechanism allows users to continue with their current task while using the device. Also, they can promptly apply solutions given by workmates in case of doubt.

- *Managing emergencies.* Unfortunately, a great number of emergencies appear in healthcare environments. These situations imply a quick response to safeguard the health of patients or residents. Ubi4health offers a mechanism to manage emergencies as quickly as possible. The application provides a button in each screen to communicate an emergency. When an employee press that button the system detects the closest workmate (who is not attending a different emergency) and sends her/him a request communicating the emergency and its location. That employee will receive the information as an alert which appears always in her/his device independently from the place where s/he is working.

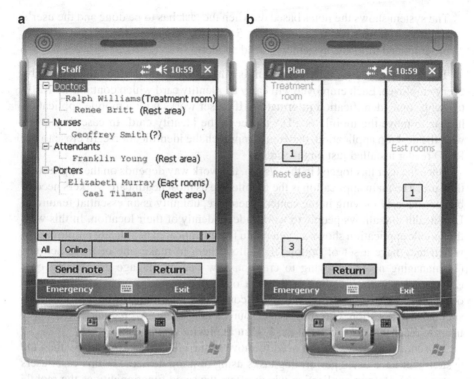

Fig. 6.3 Workmates list and residential care home map

- *Managing required information, resources and functionality to complete health-care tasks.* Ubi4health offers information that users may need in any moment, mainly users continuously moving in the residential care home. In this sense, the context-aware feature of the system proves essential. Users are able to access the information about workmates (see Fig. 6.3). The system shows a list of the workmates, where they are, what they are doing and what resources they are using. Users can filter active workmates by searching only for active users or all workmates. In the second case, the application shows in the list no active users by a question symbol instead of his location. Both lists are divided in groups according to specific health categories: physicians, nurses, auxiliary staff and porters. Additionally, the system shows a residential care home map to see where the workmates are (see Fig. 6.3). The map can be displayed floor-by-floor or zone-by-zone in each floor. The zones have a tag in their rooms which indicates the number of workers present. If a user clicks on that tags, a list with workers in that section will appear.
- *Note Management to avoid oversights.* In healthcare environments, all tasks have to be performed. This is something essential because the implications of omissions can affect the health of residents or patients. Ubi4health includes a system to eliminate oversights based on notes for employees about pending tasks.

The system shows the notes based on when the task has to be done and the user's location. If a user has to do a task in 5 m or he has forgotten to start it at the programmed time, the system will send an alert.

The first step when using the system is authentication and it has to be done by every employee. Each employee will carry an identity card which contains an RFID tag with some identification information. If a user works with a mobile application he has to move the mobile or PDA closer to the identity card. In case they work with the desktop application, they must approach the identification card close to the RFID reader installed just on the screen.

Once the user has logged in the system, the work way depends on the application they use. The main application is the mobile one as most healthcare workers need to be continuously moving in the center. Therefore, ubiquity is an essential feature in Ubi4health that allows people to work independently of their location. In this way, the mobile application shows a main menu to authenticated healthcare employees in which they have a set of options that allow them to make one of these actions: (1) managing notes, allowing to create a new one or manage an existing one; (2) managing tasks (pending or the next one); (3) communicating information to other workmates by messages; and (4) consulting information about workmates, such as their location, current tasks, resources in use, etc. All menu options allow users to reach each objective of the system as previously described.

As some employees do not need to move in the residential care home, then the system will have users performing tasks using desktop devices. In this case, users may use the desktop application which offers the same functionality as the mobile application, as described previously. However, the desktop application includes some additional functionalities oriented to supervisors. They can manage the task to be done by organizing each employee shift. Also, supervisors can see the location of each employee in order to have more information and be able to assign tasks in a better and adequate way.

6.3.3 Main Contributions of Ubi4health

Ubi4health presents some new features as compared to previous works. Most of them did not consider integrating ubiquitous, context-aware and collaborative features in a single system. This combination allows the creation of a system which works in a personalized way for each employee.

In addition, Ubi4health provides employees with a dynamic management of pending tasks. This management consists of assigning pending tasks through the collaboration of users whose context is adequate to complete them. It is an important contribution because the system is responsible for the completion of all tasks. Therefore, Ubi4health guarantees that all tasks are completed, supporting the staff who organizes each shift.

An important contribution is how the system warns employees when an emergency comes up through ubiquity and context-awareness. If a user detects an emergency in the environment, s/he sends the system a warning. Afterwards Ubi4health locates which employees are in the most adequate context to help in the emergency. That is, the system analyzes the nearest users to the emergency's location who is not assisting another emergency. Finally, the most adequate employees will receive a warning call.

This system offers a simple way of interaction; users use a PDA or a smart phone. Consequently, users will find the interaction with Ubi4health very familiar. This feature avoids problems as in MobileWARD [20] in which users are confused when interacting with the system and cannot use it correctly.

Ubi4health is supported by a simple, common and well-known network infrastructure, a WLAN. The network requires some Wi-Fi access points distributed around the environment in order to create different environment zones. The system is able to locate the employees through that simple network. It does not detect the user's exact location but an approximate point. That information is sufficient in order to know who can help somebody or is available for a specific task. This is because Ubi4health's Wi-Fi zones are designed to include small distances between the most distant points. In this way, we have not used complex techniques such as triangulation or other technologies such as Bluetooth. More specifically, [21] uses Bluetooth to locate users as this technology can detect exactly where someone is in short distances; but in large distances and under particular conditions it cannot detect users. Therefore, we did not consider Bluetooth technology because Wi-Fi gives us enough capacity to detect people in the zones we have defined as localization areas.

The infrastructure described does not imply high complexity; for example [22] requires a vast infrastructure through CISCO devices, which means higher cost than those necessary for devices that anyone can buy in computer stores. Additionally, Ubi4health's infrastructure only requires that users carry with them just a PDA, that is, only a mobile device. In healthcare environments, users may need to use many medical artifacts, so the system should not force users to take with them more than one device. In this sense, the system described in [24] implies the use of two devices, a mobile device and a bracelet.

6.4 Evaluation

The usability of Ubi4health has been evaluated based on the ISO 9126–4 standard [26]. The evaluation is focused on the efficiency, productivity and user satisfaction, as the main factors to assess the quality of the system. Effectiveness has been measured using effectiveness, task completion and error frequency. Tasks time and task efficiency has been used to measure productivity. And satisfaction has been measured using a questionnaire based on the SUS (System Usability Scale) test [27].

The evaluation is based on an experiment which challenged a group of users to perform seven concrete tasks. The group of users presented the following features:

- Ten users participated in the experiment.
- Four users were women and six men.

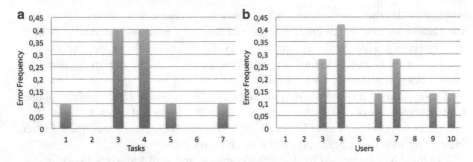

Fig. 6.4 Error frequency for each task (**a**) and for each user (**b**)

- Users' age ranged from 25 to 35 years old.
- All subjects were regular computer users.
- All of them had previously used a PDA or a touch screen mobile device. However, they had different skill levels.

Subjects were asked to perform seven tasks with the aim of using most of the features of the system. Users received some instructions about how the system works in order to be sure that they were able to complete all the tasks of the experiment. In this way, the tasks that each user had to perform were as follows:

- Task 1: log in to start the application using RFID technology. Users had to put the PDA closer to his identification card.
- Task 2: search pending tasks and identify the next one.
- Task 3: send a message to a workmate as a note. The content of the message had to be "Please, contact me".
- Task 4: read received messages and answer one. Specifically, they had to answer the oldest message.
- Task 5: search for a workmate to help you. The workmate had to be near their zone.
- Task 6: create an emergency. They were supposed to be in an emergency situation and had to call for help.
- Task 7: respond an aid request by a workmate. It appeared suddenly while they were working on the PDA.

Regarding the efficiency evaluation, Figs. 6.4 and 6.5 show error frequency (for each task and for each user) and task completion metrics, respectively. Most tasks were performed completely by the users. We identified a small error rate per user in Task 3 (0.4), Task 4 (0.4) and Task 7 (0.1). These tasks have a common sub-objective, which is to send a message to a workmate using the notes mechanism.

Their problem was finding the send button. Users had to use the scroll control to go down in the device display. In this respect we can conclude that the results indicate a high level of task completion, despite the errors found. Users learned very fast to use the Ubi4health, only with our initial introduction before beginning the experiment.

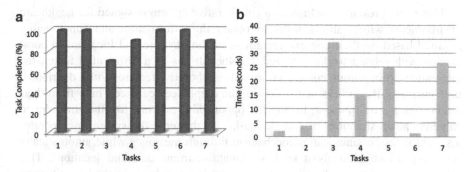

Fig. 6.5 Task completion (**a**) and task time (**b**)

The analysis of Ubi4health's productivity is based on each task time. Figure 6.5 describes average time to perform each task. Users did not spend too much time on the completion of tasks. For example, users logged in very fast using RFID technology, as shown by Task 1, with 2.03 s on average. We analyzed the standard deviation of the times (being 4.09 the maximum) and we can conclude that times were similar for all users. Additionally, the task time study shows that users learned quickly how the system worked, fact reflected by the average time in the evolution of Task 3 (33,9), Task 5 (24.95) and Task 7 (26.67). Users spent more time in Task 3 than in Task 7 despite the former is easier, which means that users learned very fast and improved their productivity.

Moving to another subject, the SUS satisfaction questionnaire, compared with ideal values, indicates that user satisfaction is really close to absolute satisfaction. SUS implies to obtain a final value with questionnaire results ranging between 0 and 100. A final value close to 100 indicates total satisfaction. In our case, the final value was 92,25; result which confirms that the participants in the experiment were highly satisfied with the use of Ubi4health.

6.5 Conclusions

Employees of healthcare centers need to collaborate in order to better achieve their objectives. Additionally, in this type of centers some employees are constantly moving around, having to use different devices based on their needs and context. However, a healthcare system should offer the same application regardless of the device type, because users generally work with the same functionality and information. This feature allows employees to familiarize with just one application, reducing their process learning time and the technological complexity. Therefore, the application should adapt its interface according to the device in such a way that the use of the distributed user interfaces paradigm becomes a requirement in healthcare systems.

This paper presents Ubi4health, a collaborative system designed for healthcare environments which allows users to obtain the information and functionality required based on their context, regardless of the daytime and location. In comparison with related works analyzed, Ubi4health has as a differential factor, the integration of ubiquitous, context-aware and collaborative features with a distributed user interface. Regardless of the device, the employees can seek help from their workmates at any moment, having the opportunity to work together in order to solve unknown situations or complex tasks. To this end, the system incorporates a synchronous communication mechanism through messages while automatically providing information about each workmate (current task and location). This information may be used to determine the workmate who is in the best situation to help. At the same time, Ubi4health uses a distributed user interface over different devices (PDA, Smartphone, mobile device, and PC) allowing users to move around the workplace. The system adapts its display mode according to the restrictions of the device.

The system has been evaluated based on the ISO 9126–4 focusing on the effectiveness, productivity and satisfaction in use. The outcomes of the evaluation indicate that (1) users learned how to use the system very easily, (2) they did not need too much time to complete each proposed task, and (3) a high level of satisfaction was achieved by all participants.

Ubi4health presents interesting future works. The authors are currently working on a new version of system, which is being developed in Android, in order to evolve and adapt the system to different devices. Additionally, we want to analyze new technologies in order to extend the capacities of the system. For example, KINECT devices can offer new possibilities to identify critical situations as falls or fainting spells.

Acknowledgments This work has been partially supported by the Spanish research project TIN2011-27767-C02-01 and the regional projects with reference PAI06-0093-8836 and PII2C09-0185-1030.

References

1. Arnrich, B., Mayora, O., Bardram, J., & Tröster, G. (2010). Pervasive healthcare, paving the way for a pervasive, user-centered and preventive healthcare model. *Methods of Information in Medicine, 1*, 67–73.
2. Bardram, J. E. (2004). Application of context-aware computing on hospital work – Examples and design principles. *2004 ACM Symposium on Applied Computing*.
3. Madeira, R. N., Postolache, O., Correia, N., & Silva, P. (2010). Designing a pervasive healthcare assistive environment for the elderly. *Ubicomp*.
4. Sneha, S., & Varshney, U. (2009). Enabling ubiquitous patient monitoring: Model, decision protocols, opportunities and challenges. *Decision Support Systems, 26*, 606–619.
5. Bick, M., & Kummer, T. (2008). Ambient intelligence and ubiquitous computing. *Handbook on Information Technologies for Education and Training*. Springer Berlin Heidelberg.

6. Cousins, K. C., & Varshney, U. (2009). Designing ubiquitous computing environments to support work life balance. *Communications of the ACM, 52*, 117–123.
7. Want, R. (2010). An introduction to ubiquitous computing. *International chapter book ubiquitous computing fundamentals*. Boca Raton: Chapman and Hall/CRC.
8. Weiser, M. (1991). The computer for the twenty-first century. *Scientific American 265*.
9. Horn, D. B., Finholt, T. A., Birnholtz, J. P., Motwani, D., & Jayaraman, S. (2004). Six degrees of Jonathan Grudin: A social network analysis of the evolution and impact of CSCW research. *ACM Conference on Computer Supported Cooperative Work* (pp. 582–591).
10. Johansen, R. (1998). *Gropware: Computer support for business teams*. New York: The Free Press.
11. Johnson-Lenz, P., & Johnson-Lenz, T. (1981). Consider the groupware: Design and group process impacts on communication in the electronic medium. In S. Hiltz & E. Kerr (Eds.), *Studies of computer-mediated communications systems: a synthesis of the findings*. Newark: Computerized Conferencing and Communications Center, New Jersey Institute of Technology.
12. Poltrock, S., & Grudin, J. (1999). CSCW, groupware and workflow: Experiences, state of arte, and future trends. In *CHI'99 extended abstracts on human factors in computing systems* (pp. 120–121). New York: ACM Press.
13. Poltrock, S., & Grudin, J. (2005). Computer supported cooperative work and groupware (CSCW). *Interact*.
14. Anagnostopoulos, T., Tsounis, A., & Hadjiefthymiades, S. (2006). Context awareness in mobile computing environments. *Wireless Personal Communications, 42*, 445–464.
15. Bricon-Souf, N., & Newman, C. R. (2007). Context awareness in health care: A review. *International Journal of Medical Informatics, 76*, 2–12.
16. Dey, A. K., & Abowd, G. (2000). Towards a better understanding of context and context awareness. *CHI*.
17. Dey, A., Abowd, G. D., & Salber, D. (2001). A conceptual framework and a toolkit for supporting the rapid prototyping of context-aware applications. *Human-Computer Interaction, 16*, 97–166.
18. Schilit, B., Adams, N., & Want, R. (1994). Context-aware computing applications. *IEEE Workshop on Mobile Computing Systems and Applications*.
19. Endsley, M. (1995). Toward a theory of situation awareness in dynamic systems. *Human Factors, 37*, 32–64.
20. Kjeldskov, J., & Skov, M. B. (2004). Supporting work activities in healthcare by mobile electronic patient records. *Computer Human Interaction, 3101*, 191–200.
21. Bardram, K., Hanse, T., Mogensen, M., & Soegaard, M. (2006). Experiences from real-world deployment of context-aware technologies in a hospital environment. *Ubicomp, 2006*, 369–386.
22. Holzinger, A., Schaupp, K., & Eder-Halbedl, W. (2008). An investigation on acceptance of ubiquitous devices for the elderly in a geriatric hospital environment using the example of person tracking. *ICCHP, Lecture Notes in Computer Science, 5105*, 22–29.
23. Favela, J., Martínez, A. I., Rodríguez, M. D., & González, V. M. (2008). Ambient computing research for healthcare: Challenges, opportunities and experiences. *Computación y Sistemas, 12*, 109–127.
24. Tentori, M., & Favela, J. (2008). Activity-aware computing for healthcare. *Pervasive Computing, 7*, 51–57.
25. Gonzales, A. L., Pollak, J. P., Retelny, D., Baumer, E. P., & Gay, G. (2011). A mobile application for improving health attitudes: Being social matters. *CHI*.
26. ISO: ISO/IEC 9126-4. (2002). Software engineering – Software product quality. *Part 4: Quality in use metrics*.
27. Brooke, J. (1996). SUS – A quick and dirty usability scale. In P. W. Jordan, B. Thomas, B. A. Weerdmeester, & A. L. McClelland (eds.), *Usability evaluation in industry* (pp. 189–194). London: Taylor & Francis.

Chapter 7
A Framework for a Priori Evaluation of Multimodal User Interfaces Supporting Cooperation

Magnus Larsson, Gilles Coppin, Franck Poirier, and Olivier Grisvard

Abstract We will present our latest research on a new framework being developed for aiding novice designers of highly interactive, cooperative, multimodal systems to make expert decisions in choice of interaction modalities given the end users, their activities and the context. Our research is conducted within the field of maritime surveillance and the next generation distributed multimodal work support in mission command centres and provide a method and tool for bridging the gap between user needs and system solution.

7.1 Introduction

The computer industry is on the brink of a new era. The future is not a solitary PC, but a diverse set of smart, cooperative devices interacting not only with its end users but also with each other while fully integrated in their environment. The interaction with these systems are multimodal where the tools become extensions of the human sensor and motor systems supporting the end users' cooperative execution of actions while trying to solve problems. The computer is thus no longer a system that just determines something by mathematical means, brings order (Fr. 'Ordinateur'), handles data (Swe. 'Dator'), count information (Hun. 'Bilgisayar'), or is a machine full of knowledge (Fin. 'Tietokone'). It is rather an infrastructure for multi-modal human-computer interaction and cooperation. However, are we as designers

M. Larsson (✉) • G. Coppin • O. Grisvard
TELECOM Bretagne, Technopôle Brest-Iroise, CS 83818, 29238 Brest Cedex 3, France
e-mail: magnus.larsson@telecom-bretagne.eu; gilles.coppin@telecom-bretagne.eu;
olivier.grisvard@telecom-bretagne.eu

F. Poirier
Lab-STICC/UMR 6285 - CNRS Université de Bretagne-Sud, BP 573, 56017 Vannes Cedex, France
e-mail: franck.poirier@univ-ubs.fr

M.D. Lozano et al. (eds.), *Distributed User Interfaces: Usability and Collaboration*,
Human–Computer Interaction Series, DOI 10.1007/978-1-4471-5499-0_7,
© Springer-Verlag London 2013

equipped to meet the rapid evolution within the computer industry? We suggest that we need to find a way to minimize the gap between analysis and design to be able to continue delivering optimized and satisfactory systems to our customers and end users at a reasonable price. Our research is being conducted in the context of ATOL (Aeronautics Technico-Operational Laboratory), a joint enterprise between TELECOM Bretagne, Thales Group and Ecole Navale (the French Naval Academy), where we study multimodal computer supported cooperative work (CSCW) within the context of maritime surveillance missions.

7.2 The Designers' Challenges of Today

The vast majority of today's expert designers are still novices within the design of highly interactive, cooperative, multimodal systems. However, they are still supposed and demanded to deliver intuitive, useful systems of high quality to a reasonable cost that optimize the total system performance. The technology necessary to create these systems are mere a mash-up of existing technologies, but the design field is quite new. Model-driven languages, methods and tools are continuously being developed and enhanced to meet the demands of the industry on adaptive, flexible and robust [1] systems designed and developed at a low cost. One example of such a project is the recently finished pan-European ITEA2: UsiXML project which is based on the $\mu 7$ concept, i.e. multi-device, multi-platform, multi-user, multi-linguality/culturality, multi-organization, multi-context, and multi-modality. However, due to the designers' lack of experience and know-how in designing these new complex systems, and due to the intended end users' and customers' inability to clarify and articulate their cooperative and multimodal needs in a comprehensive way, the designers often face infoglut resulting in poor choices in interaction modalities which lead to poor utility and usability. Some of the most common challenges are:

- The intuition and decision-making of the designers regarding multimodal computer-supported cooperative work (CSCW) environments are biased by previous experiences of single-user system design
- The complexity in group interactions and activities pose great challenges:

  - Group logistics of data collection
  - Number and complexity of variables
  - Validation of re-engineered group work

- It is time and money consuming to perform evaluation of multimodal cooperation even though one focus on a smaller set of activities and well defined user groups (even for multimodal one-user applications)
- The lowest common denominator is "easily" validated for single user systems, but not for multimodal cooperative systems with a big variety of end users
- There is a disparity in activity objective and needs between who does the work (the end users) and who gets the benefit of that same cooperative work (the customer)

One way to aid the designers would be to provide a framework that can alleviate the transition from analysis to design by directing and managing the flow of accumulated data, via analyzed information to usable knowledge and design. Today, this is a tedious time consuming work biased on deficient mental models by the designers and without any promise of quality delivered. Therefore, our intention is to help novice designers of multimodal cooperative systems to make expert decisions in choice of modality or combinations of modalities given the users, the activities and the context. We believe that this will not only enable the creation of new, for the end users, adequate intuitive systems supporting their cooperative work, but it will also optimize the ROI of projects and programs alike. In the following paragraphs we will present some aspects of an a priori evaluation framework being developed based on our understanding of human behavior and cooperation, and on how multimodal interaction could be approached to solve these issues.

7.3   Design of Multimodal CSCW Systems

What ultimately determines one's productivity is actually not as much about what tools one uses, as about how one uses them. Therefore, before we describe our new framework under development we will briefly define the context within which we imagine it to be used. As we are focusing on enhancing the work of the designers to optimize time, money and quality we recommend an agile approach due to its strengths in dealing with uncertainty and high requirements volatility in a flexible and suitable manner. [2] An agile approach provides speed, short iterations and runnable software early in the project lifecycle, but it does not necessarily secure the utility and usability of the product or service per se. Hence, we suggest that in addition to an agile approach one should also make use of a User-Centered Systems Design approach as proposed by Gulliksen and Göransson [3] thus putting the focus on the end user while providing adequate support for the designers and developers. We propose that our framework should be used as an aid throughout the development process by bridging the gap between the analysis phase and the design phase of each iteration. We propose an a priori evaluation framework intended to be used as a map, or as guidance if you may, during each iteration to help the designer transform the user needs into a system solution, thus minimizing the gap between the design model and the user's model [4].

7.4   Human Behaviour and Cooperation

Human performance is considered to be a key factor in 'total system performance' and it is recognized that enhancements to human performance will correlate directly to enhanced total system performance, and reduced life cycle costs. [5] Focusing on human performance means to focus on human behavior, i.e. human activity patterns. Notably, one of the strongest assets of human beings are their ability to interact with each other in quite complex ways in order to fulfill a great number of simultaneous individual and cooperative tasks initiated from a wide variety of intentions [6]. These interactions take place within a group of people, i.e. two or more participants, who can be considered to cooperate to the extent that they (1) consider each other cognitively in interaction, (2) have a joint purpose, (3) consider each other ethically in interaction, and (4) trust each other to act according to 1–3 [7]. Novices and experts meet in different groups within which they can take on passive, active or expansive roles [8], while belonging to different communities of interest and practice at the same time [9]. Their interactions can be collective or dispersed and they can be direct, i.e. interpersonal, or indirect, e.g. mediated by computers. Furthermore, depending on their level of involvement, one can consider them to engage in no interaction, lightweight interaction, information sharing, coordination, collaboration or cooperation. In addition, the way the end users communicate with each other and with the computer system depends on the communication channels provided, i.e. the interaction modalities or combination of modalities available. Examples of input modalities are the traditional mouse and keyboard, to the more contemporary tactile, gesture and vocal interfaces, and the emerging eye-tracking and brain–computer interface (BCI), also known as mind-machine interfaces (MMI). Evidently, the complexity of human behavior and cooperation together with the challenges posed on the designer regarding the choice of interaction modality, or combinations of modalities, demands a comprehensive framework to avoid infoglut when moving from analysis to design. Stressors caused by inadequate work environments affect our ability, willingness and opportunity to perform. Hence, what we propose is a framework that takes into account the biological, mental and contextual aspects of human behavior/activity patterns.

Based on the work of prominent scientists during mid and late nineteenth century, such as Charles Robert Darwin, Gustav Theodor Fechner and Mikhaylovich Sechenov, the Russian psychologist Lev Semyonovich Vygotsky founded cultural-historical psychology, thus closing the gap between the natural sciences and the mental sciences of human behavior. He approached behavior not as a result but rather as a process in motion and in change, i.e. by studying behavior as interaction. Vygotsky's research on activities bridged the gap between the mental and the physical contexts of human behavior and consciousness [10]. Activity Theory (AT), an evolution of Vygotsky's research, provides a basic framework for human interaction and for us a useful basic unit of analysis; the activity.

The AT concept deals with a set of fundamental types [8], which are:

- An object – Activities can be distinguished by their objects. It is the object and the transformation of that set object that drives the activity.
- A collective phenomenon – The activity does not take place in isolation but is always a collective phenomenon.
- A subject (agent) – The activity has a subject or a collective of subjects who understands the motive of the activity. In our research we refer to the subject as an actor or a role.

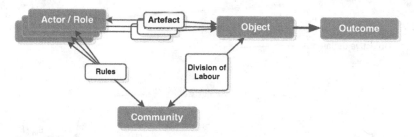

Fig. 7.1 The basic structure of a cooperative activity [11] with its properties visualized and given a relation to each other with mediating artefacts, rules and division of labour being multimodal in their character

- A material environment – The activity exists in and transforms its material environment.
- A historically developing phenomenon – The activity is a process that has a shared memory.
- Contradictions – The force behind the development of an activity are contradictions.
- Actions – Participants realize an activity through conscious and purposeful actions.
- Culturally mediated relationships

These fundamental types can easily be illustrated in a diagram together with their individual relationships. Kuutti's research [8] on AT and its fundamental types has resulted in a useful framework for research on computer-supported cooperative work. Cadier [11] extended the AT framework of Kuutti to manage both negotiation and execution of cooperative work (see Figs. 7.1 and 7.2, below), thus enabling analysis of cooperative activity.

The model in Fig. 7.1, above, depicts the 'playground' of an activity, whereas the model in Fig. 7.2, below, illustrates the actual execution process of an activity and its sub-activities/tasks and operations. Furthermore, this model also illustrates the cooperative steps of an activity where the negotiation of division of labor is the starting point, but also the result.

Based on this knowledge we can conclude that cooperation is heterogeneous where contradictions force activities [8], that it is culturally and contextually situated and that it makes use of internal as well as external communication [10], both verbal and non-verbal [7], to organize the same activities. These activities the users later execute with the help of mediating artifacts such as computer systems. We can also conclude that the level of verbal versus non-verbal communication depends on the social context of the actor/role, which are mediated via social rules and norms and the activity's division of labor. This would suggest that no person act in isolation and that one could consider all activities, if taking into account the different levels and types of human interaction and work support, as multimodal and as being either cooperative activities or task work activities [12] where the team make use of situated and distributed cognition and cognitive processes [13].

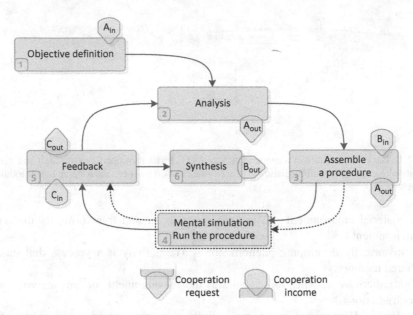

Fig. 7.2 An iterative cooperative activity process [11] where cooperative requests are multimodal acts of negotiation and decision whilst the rest of the process is multimodal (internal as well as external) actions

Based on this understanding of human interaction and CSCW we can look closer at what implications this has on the choice of interaction modalities and how we can develop a framework suitable for designers.

7.5   A Sound Choice of Interaction Modality

Human behavior, interaction and cooperation are multimodal by origin and considered natural in its essence. AT provides, as shown, a comprehensive high-level framework for organizing cooperative activities into manageable entities. However, in order to be able to provide any insight into preferred choice of multimodality for any specific context to provide a seamless natural interaction we need to enhance and develop it further. To be able to manage the cognitive aspects of the actors/roles in cooperation we can make use of Endsley's Situation Awareness (SA) model [14], which, in combination with our understanding of the human sensor and motor system provide a mind and body description of human capabilities (see Fig. 7.3, below). The actor/role has been given a physical interface in his/her motor and sensor system as well as a detailed description of his/her mental capabilities, which both take part in transforming the object mediated by an artifact, e.g. a computer system, and vice versa. The same goes for the mediated interaction with the community via cultural rules and norms. Together, the mind and body define the

Fig. 7.3 Enhanced actor/role model based on work of [8, 9, 11], and [14]

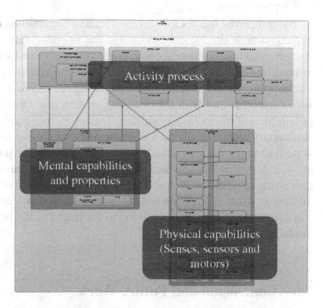

Fig. 7.4 Our latest artifact model of the computer interface based on the work of [1, 10, 15], and [16]

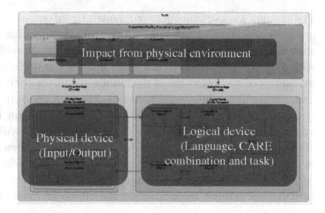

activity process from SA via decision to execution of the activity, either alone or in cooperation with other actors/roles. The actors'/roles' mental capabilities and properties are affected by the community's social and cultural rules and vice versa and the actors'/roles' use of artifacts to transform the object of interest into sought for outcome also transforms the actor/role in that same process.

A computer system also has a physical interface towards the outside world and an inner "mental" core based on the intentions of the system creators as well as its users' use and re-work (see Fig. 7.4, below). The physical aspects, i.e. input and output devices, together with the logical interaction language make an interaction modality which together with e.g. CARE properties can be combined into multimodal interactive systems [15] while providing plasticity [1] to correspond to the changing context.

By comparing the actors' different mental capabilities and properties, and their objectives with the logical device and the intended task support of the computer system, while taking into account both cooperative tasks and work tasks, one can evaluate the mental aspect of the activity, i.e. the systems cognitive properties [17]. Furthermore, by at the same time comparing the physical capabilities of the actors with each other and with the computer system one can find constraints as well as possibilities of interaction modalities. The actors' negotiation with the group and the community regarding division of labor while executing tasks aided by a computer system changes the way a task is conducted and what interaction modalities that are suitable for the overall activity as well as the execution and negotiation of the task work. In addition, if considering the impact of activity workload and external as well as internal stressors and its impact on human cognition and behavior one can design the system to correspond to the needs of the users regarding interaction modality.

7.6   Conclusion and Future Work

The continuous development of our models based on our cross-disciplinary research proves very promising. Our research on the next generation work support for tactical commanders and sensor operators within maritime surveillance, who work closely within highly specialized teams, while making use of different kinds of interaction modalities or combinations of modalities to execute their work, and who operates under stressful conditions, are well suited for our research. We hope that our results will shed some light on the impact of cooperation on the preferred choice of interaction modalities and vice versa. Our framework will be a welcome help for novice designers of cooperative multimodal systems when making expert decisions in choice of modality or combinations of modalities while designing for optimal performance. However, our research is only scratching the surface of a research field that needs much more attention and thorough investigation.

References

1. Vanderdonckt, J., et al. (2008). In D. Tzovaras (Ed.), *Multimodality for plastic user interfaces: Models, methods, and principles multimodal user interfaces* (pp. 61–84). Heidelberg: Springer.
2. Thakurta, R., & Ahlemann, F. (2010). Understanding requirements volatility in software projects-an empirical investigation of volatility awareness, management approaches and their applicability. In *System Sciences (HICSS), 43rd Hawaii International Conference on 2010*, IEEE.
3. Gulliksen, J., et al. (2003). Key principles for user-centred systems design. *Behaviour & Information Technology, 22*(6), 397–409.
4. Norman, D. A., & Draper, S. W. (1986). *User centered system design; new perspectives on human-computer interaction*. Hillsdale: Lawrence Erlbaum.

5. DOD. (1999). *Department of defense handbook: Human engineering program process and procedures*, U.S.A.A.a.M. Command, Editor. 1999: Redstone Arsenal (pp. 35898–5270).
6. Nowak, M. (2006). Five rules for the evolution of cooperation. *Science, 314*(5805), 1560–1563.
7. Allwood, J. (2001). *Cooperation and flexibility in multimodal communication cooperative multimodal communication*. In H. Bunt & R. Beun (Eds.), (pp. 113–124). Berlin/Heidelberg: Springer.
8. Kuutti, K. (1991). The concept of activity as a basic unit of analysis for CSCW research. *ECSCW'91: Proceedings of the Second Conference on European Conference on Computer-Supported Cooperative Work*. Kluwer Academic, Amsterdam.
9. Hoogstoel, F. (2001). Les répercussions du travail coopératif assisté par ordinateur sur les systèmes d'information. In C. Kolski (Ed.), *Environnements évolués et évaluation de l'IHM*, Paris: HERMES Science Europe .
10. Vygotsky, L. S. (1978). *Mind in society: Development of higher psychological processes*. Cambridge: Harvard University Press.
11. Cadier, F. (2007). Modèles Cognitifs pour les Systeme d'Aide a la Decision Collective: Application a la Patrouille Maritime. In *Département Logique des Usages, Sciences Sociales et de l'Information* (p. 192). Brest: École Nationale Supérieur des Télécommunications de Bretagne.
12. Hoc, J. M. (2001). Towards a cognitive approach to human–machine cooperation in dynamic situations. *International Journal of Human-Computer Studies, 54*(4), 509–540.
13. Woods, D. D., & Hollnagel, E. (2006). *Joint cognitive systems: Patterns in cognitive systems engineering*. Boca Raton: CRC/Taylor & Francis.
14. Endsley, M. R., & Garland, D. J. (2000). *Situation awareness analysis and measurement*. Mahwah: Lawrence Erlbaum.
15. Nigay, L. (2004). Design space for multimodal interaction. In *IFIP Congress Topical Sessions*.
16. Verdurand, E. (2011). Modélisation et Evaluation de l'Interaction dans les Systeme Multi-modaux, *In Département Logique des Usages, Sciences Sociales et de l'Information* (p. 257). Brest: Télécom Bretagne.
17. Hutchins, E., & Klausen, T. (1998). Distributed cognition in an airline cockpit. In Y. Engeström & D. Middleton (Eds.), *Cognition and communication at work* (pp. 15–34). New York: Cambridge University Press.

Chapter 8
Enhancing the Security and Usability of Dui Based Collaboration with Proof Based Access Control

Marcel Heupel, Mohamed Bourimi, Philipp Schwarte, Dogan Kesdogan, Thomas Barth, and Pedro G. Villanueva

Abstract Managing access control (AC) of shared resources is at the heart of any collaboration platform. Thereby, the usability of used AC techniques is crucial for projects with high expectations to fast response times within targeted collaboration processes. In this paper, we address the special case of using the anonymous credential system *idemix* in a project dealing with distributed user interfaces (DUIs) to enhance decision making in disaster situations. We show the potential of using *Idemix* to enhance the usability of decision making in crisis situations by using DUIs while considering security and privacy. We present this exemplary by means of a developed prototypic collaborative environment, composed by a *WallShare* based server-side and mobile application for supporting collaborative scenarios within the ReSCUeIT project. Since DUI based collaboration demands wide-support of multiple devices, especially mobile ones, we further present *IdeREST*, a REST-full *idemix* integration and *idemiX++*, the first C++ based implementation of *idemix* worldwide, to the best of our knowledge. With both we show how to overcome the current gap related to the simultaneous support on non-Java devices such as Windows Phone 7/8 along with performance improvements on Android based platforms when using *idemix* as an exemplary anonymous credential system.

M. Heupel (✉) • M. Bourimi • P. Schwarte • D. Kesdogan • T. Barth
Information Systems Institute – IT Security Group, University of Siegen, Hölderlinstr. 3, 57076 Siegen, Germany
e-mail: heupel@wiwi.uni-siegen.de; bourimi@wiwi.uni-siegen.de; schwarte@wiwi.uni-siegen.de; kesdogan@wiwi.uni-siegen.de; barth@wiwi.uni-siegen.de

P.G. Villanueva
Computer Science Research Institute, University of Castilla-La Mancha, Campus Universitario de Albacete S/N, 02071 Albacete, Spain
e-mail: pedro.gonzalez@uclm.es

M.D. Lozano et al. (eds.), *Distributed User Interfaces: Usability and Collaboration*, Human–Computer Interaction Series, DOI 10.1007/978-1-4471-5499-0_8, © Springer-Verlag London 2013

8.1   Introduction

Distributed user interfaces (DUIs) are not just gaining importance in famous science fiction movies (e.g. Minority Report, Paycheck or Avatar) but also in real life situations. The reader may remember for instance scenes from both movies where a user is moving interfaces from one screen to another screen or device. Even though the definition of DUIs is still not sharpening whereas the "*distribution*" aspect of UIs is at this time restricted to one single application, its runtime environment or used (technical) platform(s), the need of addressing emerging issues from potential dangerously situations becomes important.

The previous statements are motivated in our case from first collected experiences within a project based on distributed user interfaces to enhance "*decision making support*" at the level of UI capabilities in disaster situations. Since such situations involve various stakeholders who are collaborating to solve crisis situations, security and privacy issues must be addressed. Indeed, involved parties own different degrees of trust and access rights to sensitive information, especially when such collaboration is not just taking place in one dedicated room, but in geographically distributed situation rooms. In general, taking part in collaborative settings often demands sharing sensitive information. According to the respective collaboration scenario this could involve private and business information. Thereby, collaborative applications gain strength from leveraging efficient, secure, and privacy-respecting interaction and communication between individuals as well as seamlessly supported interaction, i.e. in terms of fast response times that make using the application an enjoyable user experience.

On the one hand, security and privacy are one of the most-cited critical aspects in pervasive and ubiquitous computing [1]. On the other hand, usability is a prerequisite for security and privacy. Therefore, it is part of a major effort to balance and improve security and privacy design of applications by considering usability aspects, especially in collaborative systems using shared workspaces. One of the most disregarded and critical topics of computer security has been and still is, the understanding of the interplay between usability and security [2]. Since accessing shared information in collaborative environments is often coupled to user identities, IBM's Identity Mixer *idemix* and proof-based credential systems in general (e.g. Microsoft's U-Prove) could ease transparently performing authorization, e.g. without any user intervention at the UI level. Thereby, they ensure minimization of disclosed information in access control transactions, because just cryptographic proofs of attribute possession (e.g. member of a disaster team) and not information attributes (e.g. name, affiliation) are being exchanged. The compromise that can be reached by using *idemix* between usability and security/privacy, however, is currently negatively affected. In fact, the integration of advanced access control technologies, namely anonymous credential systems remains currently a challenge on various platforms due to different reasons. Especially the usage of mobile platforms underlies many restrictions in this respect. Such restrictions could diminish benefits from using DUIs that demand a wide support of different platforms. Thus, we also present *IdeREST* and *idemiX++*, the first C++ based implementation of *idemix* worldwide, in order to support non-Java devices such as Windows Phone 7/8 and Android-based platforms in our scenarios.

The rest of this chapter is structured as follows. First, an overview of the state-of-the-art is given in Sect. 8.2. Next, in Sect. 8.3, we present the requirements derived from scenarios of the ReSCUeIT[1] project and related work. In Sect. 8.4 we propose our evaluation approach, before we finalize the paper with our conclusions and short description of on-going and future work in Sect. 8.5.

8.2 State-of-the-Art

Access control is an essential mechanism a system has to provide primarily in collaborative environments that manage shared resources among various users. The classical way in security systems design to manage access control is to bind access rights (permissions to access resources) to the users' identity. However, collaborative settings need some degree of user information disclosure – often related to identity attributes – in order to achieve the intended goals as Palen and Dourish mention in [3] (e.g. signing up for an account). One of the means to enhance privacy while supporting collaboration as well as communication of individuals and services is to use partial identities (e.g. pseudonyms). Partial identities consist of selected user data to be disclosed for a particular purpose and context. Even those partial identities are linked to real ones in the system design; the privacy in various interaction flows can be enhanced since linkability is made difficult. Such linkability could affect the security of processes and privacy of involved parties in some crucial scenarios. However, various problems are related to security and usability trade-offs in this respect. Experts from various research communities believe that there are inherent trade-offs between security and usability to be considered [2, 4, 5].

A fairly large number of research contributions focused on making access rights management usable for end-users. Bullock and Benford provided an overview on existing approaches for access rights management in collaborative environments in [6] and Haake et al. in [7]. Latter work reviewed the state-of-the-art especially by focusing on group formation and access control in shared workspace systems, concluding that "*in todays shared workspace systems access rights management by end-users is insufficiently supported, either due to too complex role models, access control parameters and UIs that end-users cannot easily understand, or due to insufficient functionality*". The challenges increase if (lay) users are asked to set access rights for others, delegate rights, or manage their own security and privacy preferences.

As mentioned before, proof-based anonymous credential systems own great potential to make access control more usable since they could ease transparently performing identification (of users) and authorization (to access resources),

---

[1]ReSCUeIT: Robust and secure supply-chain supporting IT. http://www.sichere-warenketten.de

e.g. without any user intervention at the level of the UI. For instance, *idemix* enables to perform anonymous authentication between users and/or service providers and as well supports accountability of transactions [8]. An *idemix* credential is obtained from an issuing authority, attesting certain attributes to the user, such as birth date, group membership or access rights and allows for various protocols and mechanisms cited in standard literature (i.e. property proofs, usage limitation, revocation of credentials, revocation of anonymity, verifiable encryption). During the issuance protocol the user and a certificate authority (CA) interactively create a credential. In contrast to privacy enhancing technologies sending pseudonym certificates to a given verifier, *idemix* based solutions only send proofs (such as "I am older than 18" or "I am working in the automotive industry"). It allows for un-linkable, selective disclosure of such attested attributes while not revealing others. When the user shows this credential to another entity (another user or a service provider), the credential itself is never revealed. Since *idemix* enables involving the user in the personal data disclosure process, the user can decide which attributes to disclose [9].

DUI technology is mostly used within collaborative environments and could also profit from proof-based credential systems to ease the distribution of respective UIs (regardless of the meaning of the distribution aspect we addressed in the introduction). However, DUIs demand a wide-support of different platforms in order to not hinder the distribution aspect and to support different interaction schemes. Especially when targeting DUI support on mobile devices, different capabilities of modern mobile devices (e.g. smart-phones and Tablet PCs), addressing security and usability aspects becomes crucial. The widely used password authentication is in general a good approach under the prerequisite that a secure password is used. In practice, used passwords are notoriously weak, mostly because of limitations of human information-processing and/or limited capabilities of the respective mobile device. A contribution from the usability field to enhance authentication is e.g. the usage of graphical passwords. An example is the usage of graphical authentication in Android smart-phones to unlock the main screen. However, also those approaches have been proven to be not secure enough e.g. due to the smudge traces that can emerge on the screen surface [10]. Biometrics also allow enhancing authentication but are still *"classified as unreliable because human beings are, by their very nature, variable"* [2, 11]. In comparison to all these approaches, proof-based anonymous credential systems could enhance DUI-based collaboration while building an acceptable compromise between usability and security in privacy-preserving collaborative scenarios.

According to Corella et al. [12], public key certificates as well as classic password-based approaches are not convenient to use on mobile device. Hence, we leverage *idemix* as a substitute for certificates, in general there is no manual interaction necessary in authorization or authentication use cases. Further we developed an approach combining idemix with OAuth [13]. Thereby no confirmation of certificates or entering of password is needed by the users (e.g. at user interface level).

Security and usability research for developing usable (psychologically acceptable) security mechanisms is a young research field, which depends on the context usage [2]. Because of this and many facts cited above, we argue that security and privacy design by considering usability is specific to the project context, and thus we focus in this contribution on concrete, ReSCUeIT-specific requirements by considering lessons learned from previous projects related to proof-based anonymous credential systems.

8.3 Scenarios and Requirements Analysis

ReSCUeIT is a joint German-French research and development project, which focuses on increasing the safety of the food supply chain for the civil population. It integrates partners from academia and industries along the food supply chain (production, retail and logistics) in order to assure consideration of requirements from all stakeholders. One goal within the scope of this project is to develop a software platform supporting the whole business process lifecycle from business process modelling to process execution. This platform needs to be fault-tolerant and scalable in order keep the supply chain working even in the face of cyber attacks on the IT infrastructure of one or several supply chain-partners.

Earlier work [14] describes the setting basing on secure DUI for supporting decision making in disaster situation. The full presentation of the ReSCUeIT requirements goes beyond the scope of this paper. However, we mention that also the usage of *idemix* in first prototypes faced restrictions. The main restriction consists in the fact that reference implementation of its specification is only provided in Java, which, in the rising era of mobile and ubiquitous computing represents a drawback for platforms, restricting the development to other languages as in the case of Apple's iOS devices or Microsoft's Windows Phone. Since some mobile platform providers only support their own programming languages (e.g. Apple and Microsoft), the usage of *idemix* has to be supported on non-Java devices with other means In general, a wider support of mobile platforms and other devices such as Tablet PCs has been required (**Requirement 1; R1**). Especially the usage of mobile platforms underlies many restrictions in this respect (i.e. supporting various mobile platforms and granting acceptable response times from the usability point of view) and could profit of potential *idemix* integration in ReSCUeIT (and other projects such as di.me[2] project). As part of a previous work an Android prototype has been implemented and analysed [15]. The main focus was on general feasibility and performance evaluation, but lab tests with end-users also identified several usability requirements. An additional analysis of selected ReSCUeIT scenarios identified the need for usability enhancements in terms of response time on Java platforms with *idemix* (s. also cited literature in [15], e.g. the work of Armac et al.) (**R2**).

---

[2]di.me: Integrated digital.me Userware. http://www.dime-project.eu

8.4 Approach

From the previous explanations, *idemix* represents a perfect starting point for automating privacy-enhancing authentication and authorization in the background. By allowing for background authentication and authorization, a good performance could be reached since no user interaction is needed. The CA could provide needed acknowledgements for access permission enforcement. However, this needs a pre-defined set of attributes, which are allowed to be included into automatic generated proofs. In the case where such attribute sets are to be changed on runtime, one can expect poor response times with increasing attributes' numbers [15].

Meeting **R1** was mainly accomplished by providing *IdeREST* as technological solution. In order to be as flexible as possible in terms of used hardware, we wanted to support many different mobile platforms, with different capabilities, we needed to find a way to perform the *idemix* protocols, even on platforms not supporting Java. We decided to provide the functionality in form of a RESTful *idemix* service. To achieve this, we externalized the computation functionality of *idemix* to a server offering a REST-API. With this server application, which we call *IdeREST,* it is now possible to use the *idemix* functionality even on Windows Phone 7, Windows server or to lower computation time for weak mobile devices. Latter represents a way to reach good performance in the case of such devices (**R2**). Another approach for reaching better performance, and to be able to perform the necessary protocols also offline (which is one of the drawbacks of IdeREST), was to port the *idemix* reference implementation to C++ (called *idemiX++*). Especially for mobile platforms and since the majority of them is Unix/Linux-based, the native support of C++ is mostly possible without big restrictions, even on iOS devices. This is also the case for many kinds of embedded systems used in privacy-sensitive scenarios. In addition, the potential of leveraging *idemix* capabilities by integrating it in Web-based applications, which are still the most used applications, also on mobile devices, becomes possible with the new tendency of supporting C/C++ for programming native browser extensions as in the case of Google Chrome (officially used as reference Web browser) (**R2**).

For demonstrating **R1**, we implemented an emergency scenario, in which different stakeholders of the supply chain, managed by ReSCUeIT need to interact in order to find a fast solution for an emerging crisis. To support interaction and sharing of documents during a crisis session, the *WallShare* [16], a DUI supporting system proved to be adequate to validate our approach [14]. So we used this as a basis for our prototype and extended it to meet our requirements in this work. *WallShare* is a platform providing users with a collaborative multi-pointer shared desktop, which is projected on a wall or displayed on a big screen. Pointer control is performed with mobile devices such as PDAs, smart phones, Tablet PCs, etc. In the implemented scenario, we make use of the *WallShare* system, in order to support the collaboration in a local meeting situation. A large *WallShare* screen is projected in a meeting room and each user has an additional screen on his/her mobile device in order to interact with *WallShare* and see additional information.

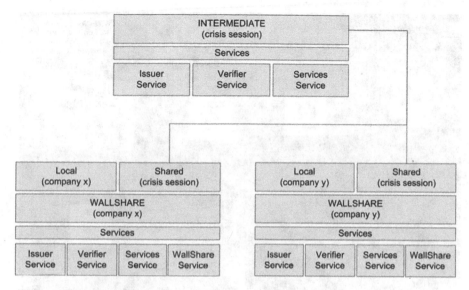

Fig. 8.1 Architecture of two WallShare instances communicating via an intermediate

Each user has an *idemix* credential, allowing proving certain characteristics, like, e.g., role, age, or employer. With this it is possible to define special access rights for each shared document and also to log in to the *WallShare* system. If a crisis situation occurs, and multiple, locally distributed, organizations need to interact, an intermediate session is instantiated (see Figs. 8.1 and 8.2).

The local *WallShare* screen will then become split into two areas, a shared area that is the same for all distributed *WallShare* instances, and a local area, only viewable by the local team. Now all participants can easily exchange important documents pictures etc. by just dragging them into the shared area. The *WallShare* servers (Windows server), as well as the mobile *WallShare* clients (Windows Phone 7) are making use of the *IdeREST* service in order to authenticate each other. When a new session is instantiated, the creator can define special access rights for the expert team to join. Thereby it is possible to make the intermediate session only accessible e.g. to managers of a certain organization and the local police department. Third parties, like, e.g., the press, can thereby excluded, which can be of high importance in delicate situations, e.g., when dealing with threats to the food supply chain. The generation of the required *idemix* proofs is performed in the background, hidden from the user. The issued credential (comparable to an virtual id card) is initially stored on the device and relevant attributes (and only them) can be shown automatically on demand. Listing 8.1 shows the code of the Windows Phone prototype used to login with *idemix* to the *WallShare* server.

With respect to **R2** and *idemiX++*, a deep analysis of the Java reference implementation, especially of the packet structure was performed (see Fig. 8.3).

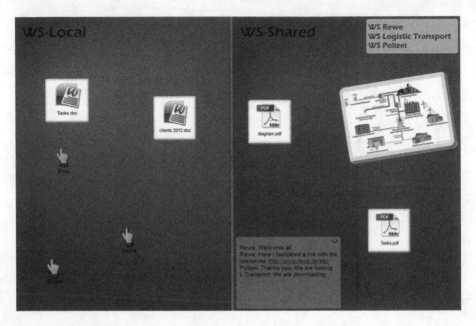

Fig. 8.2 WallShare showing a local and a shared area

```
1  private void LoginIdemix(){
     string result = client.Connect(App.Host, ECHO_PORT);
3    if (result != "Success"){
       MessageBox.Show("Error de servidor");
5      return;
     }
7    App.Socket = client;
     App.Nonce = App.Socket.Receive();
9    App.NombreProofspec = App.Socket.Receive();
     try{
11     IsolatedStorageFile store = IsolatedStorageFile.
             GetUserStoreForApplication();
       if (!store.FileExists(App.NombreProofspec)){
13       App.Proxy.DameProofSpecAsync(App.NombreProofspec);
       }
15     else{
         CompilaProof();
17     }
     } catch (Exception ex){
19       MessageBox.Show("Error con el servidor");
         App.Socket.Close();
21       return;
     }
23 }
```

Listing 8.1 Code example to the login implementation in the Windows Phone client

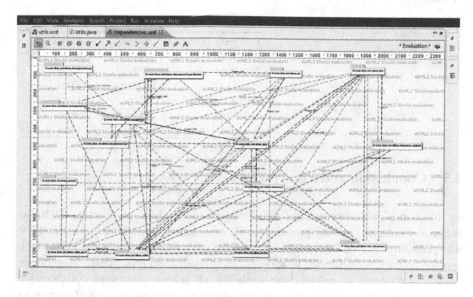

Fig. 8.3 Overview of the idemix packet structure

It was decided to more or less keep this structure for the C++ port. Thereby the porting process was more transparent and changes and updates in the Java Code can easily be adapted in the C++ version. Besides the same packet structure, C++ differs a lot from Java, so the code itself could not just be converted 1:1 but have to be written completely new. Further, the C++ implementation makes use of the Qt-framework in order to cover Java-standard Objects not covered by C++ (e.g., String, generic objects, etc.). Most important core components of *idemix* are the cryptographic algorithms for modular exponentiations, prime number generation and so on. In order to implement this for C++ we used the Crypto++ library to achieve for example randomisation and BigInteger calculation).

We performed a preliminary performance analysis, indicating a notable faster computation time. The table compares the measured computation time for the creation of selected proofs on the same platform (average of 50 measurements). The C++ implementation of *idemix* was developed to help fulfil both identified requirements (**R1** and **R2**) and could open new perspectives. That is, a C++ implementation that is much faster than the Java one as outlined in the first comparison results within Table 8.1. This will lead to shorter response times in general and could thereby improve the user experience (from the usability point of view) of *idemix*-based applications.

Table 8.1 Performance of Java versus C++ implementation

Function name	idemix java	idemix C++
TestCred0_noValues	535ms	114ms
TestCred1c	604ms	80ms
TestCred2	649ms	89ms
ProofCred0	569ms	37ms
VerifyCred0	33ms	13ms
ProofCred1a	133ms	38ms
VerifyCred1a	16ms	12ms

8.5 Conclusion and Future Work

In this paper, we presented the continuation of previous work using DUIs to enhance secure and privacy-preserving collaboration. The motivation for our work was primarily derived from scenarios needing such support within the ReSCUeIT project. Mainly, we described how DUIs could profit from proof-based anonymous credential systems to enhance the usability of access control in collaborative environments. We used *idemix* as an exemplary anonymous credential system to show this. The feasibility of our approach was demonstrated by implementing the prototype, which enables participants to transparently exchange data in the background without the need for explicit interaction (e.g. in UIs). The shortcomings of *idemix* as pure Java implementation – especially with respect to supporting various mobile platforms – were overcome by means of the *IdeREST* and *idemiX++* solutions. With both solutions, we showed how to support larger base of mobile non-Java platforms and/or to improve the performance by leveraging C++ as native language. Our approach presents a solution, which addresses the full spectrum of enhancing DUI based collaboration in various settings and with simultaneous support of different devices and platforms. Future directions intend enhancing the usability and security in P2P scenarios within the di.me project and for generating complex proofs at runtime for users without security background.

Acknowledgements This work has been partially supported by the joint project ReSCUeIT, funded by the German Federal Ministry of Education and Research (BMBF) and the French L'Agence nationale de la recherché (ANR) under grant no. 13N10964. Further support was provided by the EU FP7 project digital.me, funded by the EC (FP7/2007–2013) under grant no. 257787 as well as the Spanish CDTI research project CENIT-2008-1019, the CICYT TIN2011-27767-C02-01 project and the regional projects with reference PPII10-0300-4172 and PIIC09-0185-1030.

References

1. Hong, J. I., & Landay, J. A. (2004). An architecture for privacy-sensitive ubiquitous computing. *MobiSys'04: Proceedings of the 2nd International Conference on Mobile Systems, Applications, and Services* (pp. 177–189). ACM, New York.
2. Cranor, L., & Garfinkel, S. (2005). *Security and usability*. Sebastopol: O'Reilly Media.

3. Palen, L., & Dourish, P. (2003). Unpacking "privacy" for a networked world. *Proceedings of the SIGCHI Conference on Human Factors in Computing Systems (CHI'03)* (pp. 129–136). ACM Press, New York.
4. Shneiderman, B., Plaisant, C., Cohen, M., & Jacobs, S. (2010). *Designing the user interface: Strategies for effective human-computer interaction* (5th ed.). Reading: Addison Wesley.
5. Boyle, M., Neustaedter, C., & Greenberg, S. (2008). Privacy factors in video-based media spaces. In S. Harrision (Ed.), *Media space: 20+ years of mediated life* (pp. 99–124). Berlin: Springer.
6. Bullock, A., & Benford, S. (1999). An access control framework for multi-user collaborative environments. *Proceedings of the International ACM SIGGROUP Conference on Supporting Group Work. GROUP'99* (pp. 140–149). ACM, New York.
7. Haake, J. M., Haake, A., Schu İLmmer, T., Bourimi, M., & Landgraf, B. (2004). End-user controlled group formation and access rights management in a shared workspace system. *CSCW'04: Proceedings of the 2004 ACM Conference on Computer Supported Cooperative Work* (pp. 554–563). ACM Press, Chicago, 6–10 Nov 2004.
8. Camenisch, J., & Van Herreweghen, E. (2002). Design and implementation of the idemix anonymous credential system. *CCS'02: Proceedings of the 9th ACM Conference on Computer and Communications Security* (pp. 21–30). ACM, New York.
9. Bichsel, P., & Camenisch, J. (2010). Mixing identities with ease. In E. De Leeuw, S. Fischer-Hühner, & L. Fritsch (Eds.), *IFIP working conference on policies: Research in identity management (IDMAN'10)* (pp. 1–17). Springer.
10. Aviv, A. J., Gibson, K., Mossop, E., Blaze, M., & Smith, J. M. (2010). Smudge attacks on smartphone touch screens. *Proceedings of the 4th USENIX Conference on Offensive Technologies. WOOT'10, Berkeley* (pp. 1–7). USENIX Association.
11. Kryszczuk, K., & Drygajlo, A. (2008). Credence estimation and error prediction in biometric identity verification. *Signal Processing, 88*(4), 916–925.
12. Corella, F., & Lewison, K. (2012). Strong and convenient multi-factor authentication on mobiles devices.
13. Schwarte, P., Bourimi, M., Heupel, M., Kesdogan, D., Gimenez R., Wrobel, S., & Thiel, S. (2013). Multilaterally secure communication anonymity in decentralized social networking. To appear in: *Proceedings of the 10th International Conference on Information Technology: New Generations (ITNG)*, Las Vegas.
14. Barth, T., Fielenbach, T., Bourimi, M., Kesdogan, D., & Villanueva, P. (2011). Supporting distributed decision making using secure distributed user interfaces. In J. A. Gallud, R. Tesoriero, & V. M. Penichet (Eds.), *Distributed user interfaces* (Human-computer interaction series, pp. 177–184). London: Springer.
15. Heupel, M. (2010). *Porting and evaluating the performance of idemix and tor anonymity on modern smartphones*. Master's thesis, University of Siegen.
16. Villanueva, P. G., Gallud, J. A., & Tesoriero, R. (2010). WallShare: A multi-pointer system for portable devices. *AVI'10: Proceedings of the International Conference on Advanced Visual Interfaces*, ACM Request Permissions.

Chapter 9
Enhancing LACOME to Consider Privacy and Security Concerns

Sukhveer Dhillon and Kirstie Hawkey

Abstract In this chapter, we introduce LACOME, the Large Collaborative Meeting Environment, which is a collaboration system that allows multiple users to simultaneously publish their computer desktops (workspace) and/or windows on a large shared display via a network connection. We discuss the design challenges of such systems for distributed environments. We conducted a series of focus groups to obtain feedback on the initial design of LACOME. Based on our findings, we developed high level design requirements for future iterations and made recommendations to improve the design of collaborative systems; these include the need for addressing privacy and security concerns when moving from a co-located setting to a mixed presence environment.

9.1 Introduction

Large displays have been used in meeting and workspace environments over the last couple of decades. Traditionally, meetings have been run in a one-operator-per-display paradigm where a single user physically connects his/her computer to the large screen display to make it visible to other meeting participants. While this approach works well for some types of meetings (e.g., presentations with a single presenter), a more flexible system is required to support a wider variety of collaboration patterns. In particular, current tools offer poor support for meetings with multiple presenters. LACOME aims to solve this problem by enhanced ad hoc collaborative meeting support. LACOME, the Large Collaborative

S. Dhillon • K. Hawkey (✉)
Computer Science, Dalhousie University, 6050 University Avenue, PO BOX 15000,
Halifax NS B3H 4R2, Canada
e-mail: sdhillon@cs.dal.ca; hawkey@cs.dal.ca

M.D. Lozano et al. (eds.), *Distributed User Interfaces: Usability and Collaboration*,
Human–Computer Interaction Series, DOI 10.1007/978-1-4471-5499-0_9,
© Springer-Verlag London 2013

Fig. 9.1 Screenshot of LACOME system showing three shared displays on a large screen

Meeting Environment, was initially developed at University of British Columbia (see [1] and [2] for details of its development history and architecture). LACOME is a collaborative system that can be used in a meeting environment with a large screen, and was developed for use in co-located collaborative settings (Fig. 9.1).

LACOME was initially designed for use in a co-located meeting environment; however, our research goal was to expand its use to mixed presence settings. This extension was needed to support the distributed nature of meeting types. Distributed meetings have become common and can offer more flexibilities and functionalities in terms of location and time to the users [3].

LACOME provides a cross-platform, light-weight, setup-free client for end users to easily take part in collaborative interaction with a large shared display. The LACOME system supports two types of interaction through the LACOME client: (1) window management tasks on the shared display such as move, resize, iconify, and deiconify and (2) interaction at the application level through virtual network computing (VNC) servers. VNC server is an industry-standard tool for controlling a computer remotely. Users of LACOME are free to use any standard VNC server of their choice. LACOME provides input redirection through client – server architecture. Users run the LACOME Client on their machines; it captures their mouse and keyboard and forwards them to the LACOME Server. While interacting with the shared display, the system cursor on a user's own machine becomes locked and a virtual cursor appears on the large shared display connected to the LACOME server.

9.2 Related Work

As our research focus was to consider extending the use of the LACOME system for mixed presence meeting scenarios, the main focus of this related work is on distributed collaborative and electronic meeting systems.

9.2.1 LACOME as a Distributed Group Support System

Distributive Group Support Systems allows communication anywhere/anytime to support group discussion and decision making. Distributed user interfaces provide enhanced interaction capabilities to users by distributing user interface elements across users, platforms, environments and different contexts [4]. The LACOME system is an example of a distributed user interface system as it includes the following dimensions of distributed systems:

- Multiple users: The LACOME is a multiuser system as any number of users can collaborate at the same time.
- Multiple computing environments: The LACOME system is being extended for use in mixed presence collaboration (collocated and remote).
- Multiple domains and tasks: As each user is interacting with his/her personal machine, users have the flexibility of performing independent tasks and can publish their workspace for others to view and/or interact with when they deem it appropriate.
- Multiple platforms of usage: Users collaborate with different machines (laptop/desktop), hence different computing powers and platforms (operating systems).

We have identified some distributed systems that are closely related to the functionality of the LACOME system. Liveboard [5] is a large interactive display system that supports group meetings, presentations, and remote collaboration. It is a directly interactive, stylus based, large area display for meeting environments. It is fully network supported and can be used in a shared mode between remote locations. Liveboard incorporates an accurate cordless pen that allows participants to interact directly with the display which provides a natural point of focus for meetings. The Argo system [6] was another system which was designed to allow medium-sized groups of users to collaborate remotely from their desktops. The main purpose of Argo is to provide effective collaboration to remote users, modeling face to face meetings as closely as possible. In order to support remote collaboration, Argo provides three basic types of functionalities: real time digital audio and video support, general sharing of arbitrary single-user applications and groupware, and telepointing/telepainting tools for gesture and annotation in any shared window. Like the Argo system, unrestricted access in the original LACOME system would be a great challenge in distributed meeting environments.

Wallshare [7] is a collaborative system for portable devices which has similarities with the LACOME system. It is a multi-pointer system based on a client/server architecture that allows collaboration for face-to-face meetings and working groups. Therefore, connected participants can upload and download various resources to and from the shared zone. Users can collaborate through the shared zone via their mobile devices, and to use the shared zone, users have their own cursors that allow them to share any type of files, such as images, or documents. LACOME and WallShare have a number of similarities: both are distributed user interface systems and have similar functionality (i.e., client-server architecture, large display sharing, and support multi-user interaction). Dynamo [8] is another large publicly accessible multiuser interactive surface. It allows cooperative sharing and exchange of media remotely. It also supports shoulder to shoulder (collocated) collaboration by allowing multiple users to interact simultaneously on a large shared display. Users can attach multiple USB mice and keyboards to the surface and manage it as a communal resource by claiming areas of the interactive surface for use. Both Dynamo and WallShare are mainly designed for displaying and exchanging information in collaborative environments, while LACOME was mainly developed to support large collaborative meetings by screen sharing and eliminate the need to sequentially display and interact with information on a large shared display.

9.3   Design Challenges in Large Screen Distributed Collaborative Systems

There are three main aspects of the large screen distributed collaborative systems: large screen display surface, support for multi-user collaboration, and use in distributed environments. The current research challenges addressed in this chapter as we continue to refine and develop LACOME can be divided into three subsections; mixed presence challenges, privacy issues with a large shared display, and access control in a collaborative environment.

9.3.1   Collaboration Challenges in Mixed Presence Environment

Mixed presence collaboration combines distributed and collocated collaboration. The LACOME system was originally designed for collocated collaboration, but it can also be used in a mixed presence scenario with the addition of conferencing (audio, video) support to provide the necessary verbal communication. We are in the process of extending this current system to provide equal opportunities for mixed presence collaboration. Therefore, it will face all challenges typical of distributive environments.

Workspace awareness has been studied in both collocated and distributed settings. Gutwin defined workspace awareness as the up-to-the-minutes update about another's interaction with the workspace, which enables users to work more effectively [9]. When collaboration moves from a face to face setting to distributed groupware environments, many elements/attributes change in this process that makes it harder for people to maintain equality in their collaboration. We considered two attributes: environmental shrink and communication because these two play an important role and affect collaboration.

Environmental Shrink

In collocated collaboration with large wall displays (the environment LACOME has been designed to support), people generally have a good visibility of the actual physical workspace. Meanwhile, the workspace drastically shrinks for viewing on a small computer screen in distributed environments.

Communication

Communication is one of the main mechanics of collaboration for shared-workspace groupware; it includes small-scale actions and interactions that group members must perform in order to get a task done in a collaborative environment [9]. Collocated collaborators can use hand gestures to uniquely communicate significant information [10], which may be missed by remote users. One disadvantage for remote collaborators is that the collocated participants have the ability to control (i.e., stop or minimize) another individual's actions while interacting with the system through verbal communication, gestures, etc., while remote users have limited control when collaborating with the system. Co-located participants use hand gestures to put ideas in practice, to draw the attention of the group during collaboration, and to reference objects on the work surface; these cannot be obtained as easily for remote collaborators who may be limited to just a mouse cursor in remote case [11]. Although, verbal communication can be achieved through audio/video conferencing, gestural communication remains as a challenge in remote collaboration.

9.3.2   Privacy Issues in Large Shared Display

Privacy concerns arise when people share personal information on a large shared display. Visual privacy issues can increase in a large screen sharing environment where the information is more visible. In collocated meetings, privacy issues can be mitigated by social norms [12]. However, with the inclusion of remote participants, these concerns can increase. When using large screens to share information, there is a greater possibility of disclosure of confidential information to others that may cause privacy concerns. These privacy concerns are justified with empirical studies. For example, for a given visual angle and similar legibility, individuals are more likely to read text on a large screen than on a small screen [13]. There are very few frameworks that support users in preserving their privacy while sharing information on a large screen. There were no explicit privacy controls implemented in the original LACOME system; instead it relies on the social privacy norms inherent in face-to-face collaboration to allow its user to manage their privacy. As we move to implement privacy and security controls more formally, we are guided by the Social Translucence design principles [14] of providing visibility, awareness, and accountability in the system.

9.3.3   Access Control Requirements in Collaborative Systems

Since computer systems have been used for multiple applications and by multiple users, data security issues among the users have occurred. In the early days of computer use, access control mechanisms were based on the access matrix model (Lampson, 1971). These mechanisms were suitable for centralized computer systems where each user could create his/her objects and assign access rights. These mechanisms do not meet the needs of today's decentralized dynamic computing environment.

Access control is an indispensable part of any information sharing system. Collaborative environments introduce new requirements for access control, which cannot be met by using existing models developed for non-collaborative domains. Recently, there has been much research done in facilitating collaboration work among distributed groups. However, there has been little work done in controlling access to the collaboration. In fact most collaborative systems expect access to be controlled by social norms [15]. This is effective to some extent for collocated collaboration, but it is more difficult in mixed presence meeting environments.

9.4   Design Requirements to Enhance Privacy and Security in Collaborative Systems

We conducted a series of focus groups to obtain feedback on the initial design of the LACOME system in order to understand the design requirements before further developing the system. Based on our findings, we generated several requirements for LACOME and other collaborative systems to not only enhance the usability for co-located users but to also expand the privacy and security features as remote users are considered. We discuss these high level design requirements next.

9.4.1   Enhanced Workspace Awareness

Often a large number of windows will be simultaneously displayed on the large screen during a meeting with LACOME. Each window contains the published computer desktop of a user. The virtual cursor may be used to manipulate windows through such actions as moving, resizing, and iconifying. A user may take control of a window in order to interact with its contents. Our participants found it difficult to identify the workspace of other people when more than two users were sharing their desktops on the large screen. Systems like LACOME do not rely on workarounds such as time-sharing the system cursor. Each published desktop within LACOME supports one cursor to interact and control shared workspace. Other users will not know who the cursor belongs to. Thus, enhanced awareness of participants' interactions are required when a large number of people are collaborating using a system like LACOME.

9.4.2   Provide Post-session Awareness

People collaborate and share their desktop or files during a meeting by using collaborative systems. We found that our focus groups participants sought post-session awareness to know if anything has been changed in their system during the meeting, especially in a scenario when someone leaves the meeting for a short period of time. The system should save a session history so that if someone accessed other user's workspace it could be identified later.

9.4.3   Provide Access Control

There is an access control framework to connect to LACOME. It authenticates users and establishes secure connections, but once the connection is established, there is no further control on access. A user can interact with any workspace and make changes, and the owner of the associated workspace will have no control to stop it other than unpublishing the display. Our focus groups participants expressed that permission should be assigned for each new session, and access control requirements for navigation or controller should depend on the task/information and type of meeting scenario. Access permission can also be assigned at run time as well, but assigning permission at run time may interrupt discussion.

9.4.4   Provide Communication Channels

A user in a collocated meeting can communicate a significant amount of information through gestures; for example, to ask if it is permissible to move or resize the user's window, they may simply gesture or whisper to each other. In a distributed meeting, they must use a separate communication channel shared between all meeting participants (i.e., a telephone conference call or video conferencing call). In our focus groups study, participants suggested that it would be helpful to add a voice system for remote participants so that they could communicate more easily.

9.5 Proposed Design Solutions

Several new features were added to the LACOME Client; these were intended to make the software easier to use. Users are now provided with more information through tooltips and enhanced awareness of the users controlling cursor and screen. We also deployed access control to provide more security and privacy into the existing system. In this section, we discussed in detail how we implemented access control and enhanced awareness features.

9.5.1 Provide Security Controls and Visibilities of Access Control

Our focus was to provide users with controls to assign permission to access their computer. This can be done at the beginning of the meeting or at runtime. We felt that it is extremely important to include both mechanisms. The first mechanism is important because users can assign permission at the beginning of a meeting, which will reduce overhead during the meeting. If they are not sure what to assign at the start of the meeting, they can assign during the meeting. The second mechanism is important for situations in which users do not know at the beginning of the meeting who would need to interact with the content on their computer; this suggests a need for runtime permissions so that a user would be able to send an access request to obtain permission. Messages used in access control conversations include three parts: user name, IP address and port number. The user name is sent by each user to the LACOME Server and is mainly used to identify users during a meeting. The IP address and port numbers are used mainly to provide enhanced information.

Assigning Permission at the Start of a Meeting

We next provide a scenario to illustrate the assignment of permissions at the start of the meeting. In this scenario, two users – Main Computer and Vaio User – are connected with the LACOME system. When a third user – Gvlab – connects through LACOME Client, a message appears which allows the new user (Gvlab) to grant access at the beginning of the session for the other users (Main Computer and Vaio User) to interact with his display. The user can chose "Grant Access" to allow the other users to access the system or "Deny for Now" to select it later (Fig. 9.2).

Fig. 9.2 Screen prompting to allow access at the beginning of the session

Fig. 9.3 Requesting access from a user

Fig. 9.4 Requested for access by other user

Assigning Permission at Run Time

Permission can also be assigned at runtime. If a user wants to access another user's computer, a request will be sent to ask for permission. If the requested user allows "grant access", then the requester can take control of the requested computer. Otherwise, a message will come back to the requester stating that the requested user did not allow access the system.

In this scenario, Gvlab requests access from Vaio User by clicking Vaio's desktop. Two different messages will appear on the requested (Vaio User) and requestor (Gvlab) users' systems. In Fig. 9.3, a message appears on the requester's screen with the requested user name, IP address and port number.

At the same time, as shown in Fig. 9.4, Vaio User gets a message stating that Gvlab wants to access his/her system and is provided with the options to grant access or deny the request. If Vaio User presses "Grant Access", then Gvlab will

Fig. 9.5 Notification to
requester if access is denied

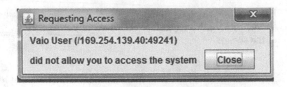

Fig. 9.6 Workspace showing
user name in window title
pane

Fig. 9.7 Screen showing
LACOME cursor labeled
with user name

be able to gain access. Otherwise, as shown in Fig. 9.5, a message will goes back
to Gvlab stating that Vaio User did not allow access to the system and will halt the
communication. If a user wants to access it again, a new communication will start
from the beginning.

If a user grants access to another user, the LACOME Server will save it for that
particular session, which means that even if the user disconnects while the other user
is still connected, the next time the user connects during that same session, he/she
will not need to ask for permission again.

9.5.2 Enhanced Workspace Awareness

It was not easy to identify the workspace of other people when more than two
users were sharing their desktops on a large screen. We noticed during the focus
group study that participants were not able to identify the cursors and workspaces
of others. We therefore decided to implement enhanced awareness features before
conducting study with further groups (Figs. 9.6 and 9.7).

Each LACOME user has one cursor to interact with and control the shared
workspaces. Thus, multiple mouse cursors appear on the large screen at any given
time. Although cursors are colour-coded for each user in the original LACOME
system, the owner of the cursor is not clear. This can be resolved by having a list
of all users and associated cursors on one side of the large screen. This technique

may work well with a few users. However, if there are a large number of users, there will be a long list, which could make it harder for users to see who is controlling or moving their shared window. We chose to label the cursor with the user name.

9.6   Conclusions

LACOME was originally designed to support collocated collaborative meetings. The system allows multiple users to concurrently publish and share their personal computer displays onto a large shared display space and to interact with each other content. It can also be used in a typical meeting room, such as a professional or an academic workplace that is augmented with a large shared display. We extended the system to consider privacy and security concerns. For this purpose, we conducted a series of focus groups to obtain feedback on the initial design of the system. Based on our findings, we developed high level design requirements for future iterations of LACOME; these include the need for addressing privacy and security concerns when moving from the use of LACOME in a co-located setting to the overarching goal of its use in a mixed presence environment. We implemented new features that provide enhanced awareness of users' shared workspaces and the interactions of others with them. We also developed an access control framework in the system that allows users to assign permissions on an ad-hoc basis. As reported in [16] we undertook an initial evaluation of the LACOME system to evaluate the overall system and the changes that we made to it. Future work will further refine the design of LACOME for mixed presence collaboration. With the addition of new access control features, LACOME can be applied to other domains, such as professional and confidential meeting environments.

References

1. MacKenzie, R. (2010). LACOME: Early evaluation and further development of a multi-user collaboration system for shared large displays. Master's thesis. The University of British Columbia.
2. Liu, Z. (2007). Lacome: A cross-platform multi-user collaboration system for a shared large display. Master's thesis. The University of British Columbia.
3. Koehne, B., & Redmiles, D. *Gaze awareness for distributed work environments*. Institute for Software Research University of California, Irvine.
4. Elmqvist, N. (2011). Distributed user interfaces: State of the art. *Proceedings of CHI Workshop on Distributed User Interfaces* (pp. 7–13).
5. Elrod, S., Bruce, R., et al. (1992). Liveboard: A large interactive display supporting group meetings, presentations, and remote collaboration. *Proceedings of the SIGCHI Conference on Human Factors in Computing Systems*. ACM Press, Monterey.
6. Gajewska, H., Kistler, J., Manasse, M., & Redell, D. (1994). Argo: A system for distributed collaboration. *Proceedings of Multimedia'94*, San Francisco.

7. Villanueva, P. G., Tesoriero, R., & Gallud, J. A. (2010). Multi-pointer and collaborative system for mobile devices. *Proceedings of Mobile HCI'10* (pp. 435–438), ACM Press.
8. Izadi, S., Brignull, H., Rodden, T., Rogers, Y., & Underwood, M. (2003). Dynamo: A public interactive surface supporting the cooperative sharing and exchange of media. *UIST'03* (pp. 159–168), ACM Press.
9. Gutwin, C., & Greenberg, S. (2000). The mechanics of collaboration: developing low cost usability evaluation methods for shared workspaces. *Proceedings of IEEE Wetice* (pp. 92–103).
10. Tang, J. (1991). Findings from observational studies of collaborative work. *International Journal of Man–Machine Studies, 34*(2), 143–160.
11. Hayne, S., Pendergast, M., & Greenberg, S. (1993). Implementing gesturing with cursors in group support systems. *Journal of Management Information Systems, 10*(3), 43–61.
12. Hawkey, K., & Inkpen, K. M. (2007). PrivateBits: Managing visual privacy in web browsers. In *Proceedings of graphics interface 2007 (GI '07)* (pp. 215–223). New York: ACM. doi: 10.1145/1268517.1268553. http://doi.acm.org/10.1145/1268517.1268553
13. Tan, D. S., & Czerwinski, M. (2003). Information voyeurism: social impact of physically large displays on information privacy. *Extended Abstracts of the ACM Conference on Human Factors in Computing Systems (CHI'03)* (pp. 748–749).
14. Grudin, J. (2001). Partitioning digital worlds: Focal and peripheral awareness in multiple monitor use. *Proceedings of CHI '01* (pp. 458–465), Seattle.
15. Giot, R., El-Abed, M., & Rosenberger, C. (2009). GREYC keystroke: A benchmark for keystroke dynamics biometric systems. *IEEE 3rd International Conference on Biometrics: Theory, Applications, and Systems (BTAS '09)* (pp. 1–6).
16. Dhillon, S. (2013). *Enhancing LACOME to consider privacy and security concerns.* Master's thesis, Dalhousie University.

Chapter 10
Evaluating Usability and Privacy in Collaboration Settings with DUIs: Problem Analysis and Case Studies

Fatih Karatas, Mohamed Bourimi, Dogan Kesdogan, Pedro G. Villanueva, and Habib M. Fardoun

Abstract The construction of mature products considering needs of end-users leads to several challenges. Especially if various experts are involved in the evaluation of prototypes being built towards a final product, an efficient support becomes crucial. In this contribution we address how such a process could be efficiently performed by means of DUI technology. We address this primarily for our case studies concerned with evaluating privacy and its usability in collaborative settings. The main idea thereby focuses on the involvement of end-users and respective usability and security experts in co-located or distributed settings. We analyze two case studies (i.e. end-user driven cloud deployment and SocialTV) and discuss our findings. The chosen case studies reflect the advantage of two-sided DUI's for collaboration support, namely, how to collaboratively evaluate usability of security and privacy measures in prototypes, which in their turn could have a collaborative nature.

F. Karatas (✉) • M. Bourimi • D. Kesdogan
Information Systems Institute – IT Security Group, University of Siegen, Hölderlinstr. 3, Siegen 57076, Germany
e-mail: karatas@wiwi.uni-siegen.de; bourimi@wiwi.uni-siegen.de; kesdogan@wiwi.uni-siegen.de

P.G. Villanueva
Research Institute of Informatics, University of Castilla-La Mancha, Campus Universitario de Albacete S/N, 02071 Albacete, Spain
e-mail: pedro.gonzalez@uclm.es

H.M. Fardoun
Information Systems Department, King Abdulaziz University (KAU), Jeddah, Saudi Arabia
e-mail: hfardoun@kau.edu.sa

M.D. Lozano et al. (eds.), *Distributed User Interfaces: Usability and Collaboration*,
Human–Computer Interaction Series, DOI 10.1007/978-1-4471-5499-0_10,
© Springer-Verlag London 2013

10.1 Introduction

Software systems and applications supporting collaboration are considered as socio-technical systems in the Human-Computer Interaction (HCI), IT Security, and Computer Supported Collaborative Work (CSCW) research fields (cf. [1–3]). Such systems are primarily difficult to design, develop, and maintain because of the socio-component related to human factors which are classified to be non-deterministic [4] (see also Chap. 7 for a detailed discussion). From this point of view, human factors (related to developers, end-users etc.) and inherent involvement of the socio-aspect makes the significance and impact of human factors in the development of collaborative applications more crucial than in other Information Systems and Information Technology (IS/IT) projects.

Nowadays, various user-centered and participatory design methodologies are followed when building sophisticated socio-technical systems, i.e. collaboration and social interaction software. Nevertheless, the problem of considering a plethora of different functional, as well as nonfunctional requirements (N/FRs) remains unsolved and gains in importance when engineering state-of-the-art software [4]. In our case, we follow AFFINE,[1] a Scrum-based methodology, which was explicitly designed to provide an alternative solution to over-complex design- and development-processes and still considering all kinds of NFRs early enough in the process along with human factors. Indeed, AFFINE focuses on earlier end-users' and experts' involvement along with developers in the process [5]. Due to the supported agility both, end-users and experts, are able to frequently evaluate developed prototypes towards a mature final product. Thus, adequately supporting collaborative evaluation of such prototypes becomes crucial.

In this contribution we show how distributed user interfaces (DUIs) technology could ease the evaluation of NFRs in collaborative settings. Due to the increasing importance of privacy [4] and its usability evaluation [2], an identified challenge in our case is to support multi-disciplinary research activities related to it (e.g. rapid prototyping or interaction design evaluation) in a collaborative way (e.g., for SocialTV or Cloud Computing scenarios). Design and evaluation of security, privacy and usability as NFRs faces various challenges especially for socio-technical systems. Therefore, the chosen case studies in this contribution reflect the advantage of two-sided DUI's for collaboration: (1) how to collaboratively evaluate usability of security and privacy in prototypes, (2) which in their turn support the interaction in collaborative settings.

The rest of this contribution is structured as follows. First we present the requirements derived from scenarios of various projects we took part in. Next we present our evaluation approach. In Sect. 10.4 we address related work. Finally we conclude in Sect. 10.5.

---

[1] Agile Framework For Integrating Non-functional requirements Engineering

10.2 Scenarios and Requirements Analysis

Our problem analysis is based on identified requirements from two different projects which we will introduce in the following:

1. The interdisciplinary SocialTV[2] project: a research cooperation of people from different faculties from the University of Siegen, Germany and the University of Castilla-La Mancha, Spain. Involved faculties are Media Sciences, Marketing, IT Security Management and Human-Computer Interaction. The goal is to develop innovative concepts for collaborative TV settings. For this purpose, different ethnographic approaches are employed such as different lab and field-tests using different SocialTV solutions involving people of various ages and expertise.
2. The ReSCUeIT[3] project: a joint German-French research and development project, which focuses on increasing the safety of the food supply chain for the civil population. It integrates partners from academia and industries along the food supply chain (production, retail and logistics) in order to assure consideration of requirements from all stakeholders. One goal, within the scope of this project, is to develop a software platform supporting the whole business process lifecycle from business process modeling to process execution. This platform needs to be fault-tolerant and scalable in order keep the supply chain working even in the face of cyber-attacks on the IT infrastructure of one or several supply chain-partners.

Earlier work [6, 7] describes the setting using DUI technology for supporting SocialTV and "*Decision Making*" in disaster situations within ReSCUeIT. In this contribution, the continuation of our work concerns the following scenarios.

The major problem scope in the SocialTV scenario in general was in the context of the navigation component. Further discussions with test participants revealed, that rapid prototyping combined with auxiliary facilities such as charts, proved insufficient for simulating real situations. On the other hand, the development of further prototypes yielded infeasible in terms of development costs and restrictions. Furthermore, the web-based prototype yielded insufficient for purposes of observing and evaluating high-fidelity capabilities. For instance, researchers demanded for facilities, which would allow them to observe geographically distributed groups, watching the same TV content. This required (among others) shared displays, which would allow being flooded with the same TV content of geographically distributed users. However, special hardware solutions offering this kind of facility are quite expensive and do not allow for reacting on emerging changes by e.g. rapid prototyping. Another issue is that such hardware does not support research needs such as security and privacy (s. [8] for further details).

In the ReSCUeIT cloud deployment scenario the efficiency of the User Interface (UI) is a crucial factor for enabling the members of the crisis team to react on

---

[2]http://www.wiwi.uni-siegen.de/itsec/forschung/projekte/socialtv.html
[3]ReSCUeIT: Robust and secure supply-chain supporting IT. http://www.sichere-warenketten.de

Fig. 10.1 Prototype for a SocialTV setting

emergency situations quickly and accurately. An important requirement is therefore testing the usability of the UI, not only in simulations, but also in real emergency situations. To reduce the danger of version conflicts, which might lead to system failures and delays in the process of *"Decision Making"* among the emergency team members, facilities are needed to ensure that all changes to the UI are immediately delegated to all clients. From a usability testing perspective, this would also increase the quality of gathered usability data and thus improvements of the UI would be more accurate. Therefore, in order to avoid that users change their behavior during observation, this aspect must be as minimal invasive as possible. Furthermore, in order to increase the flexibility of the emergency team without requiring members to collocate, facilities need to be implemented such that the emergency team can operate from virtually any environment, including their natural working environment. Currently we are using a high-level representation for security properties (see Fig. 10.1 in [7]). For a given application (which needs to be prepared in the forehand as an image containing a software stack) and cloud service which follows the Infrastructure-as-a-Service (IaaS) model, the user can determine the importance of each of the security properties confidentiality, integrity and availability on a scale with three stars where one star means "low importance" and three starts "high importance". More experienced and expert users can define security requirements at a more fine-grained level. For instance, the security property "availability" can be further divided into "response time" and "uptime". While the "stars" representation of lay users is transformed into concrete values for more fine-grained security properties based upon security best practices, experienced and expert users can define these values on their own. These requirements are then transformed into image- and cloud service-configurations in a model-driven fashion [9].

For accuracy and in summary, the analysis of various scenarios from both projects, representing contrary use cases from leisure and professional life, yields three requirements (**R1** to **R3**):

1. Facilities for evaluating (i.e. field testing) deployed solutions in simulated as well as real situations (**Requirement 1; R1**)
2. Flexible, parallel interaction of involved users with changes to the UI taking effect immediately for all users (**R2**)
3. Live observation facility from **R1** should influence users as less as possible in order to assure that users behave natural (**R3**)

10.3   The WallShare Platform Based Approach

To fulfill our requirements **R1-R3**, we extended the WallShare platform [10]. WallShare provides users with a collaborative multi-pointer shared desktop that is projected on a wall, or displayed on a big screen (**R1, R2**). Pointers are controlled through mobile devices, such as PDAs, smart-phones, tablet PCs, etc. using dragging gestures over the mobile device screen (**R2**). Here, the mobile devices act as remote controls that can be adapted easily to new situations (**R3**). The system allows users to upload, or download resources to/from the shared desktop using a pointer that is controlled from the users' mobile devices by means of gestures over the screen (**R1**). All UI templates are managed centrally and then served to any kind of display. Changes on the template are taking effect on the displays immediately. No update of mobile phone clients is needed (**R2**).

The resulting system contributes to usability and collaboration in two ways:

1. It improves collaboration between users and observers by not dictating any mode of interaction. Members from both groups can work either collocated or distributed and are not bound to any physical location.
2. Awareness of users is addressed by not showing any observer functionality if no observer is present at the same location. This reduces irritations, possible wrong usage and thus increases the quality of observation data.

From the interactive perspective, according to the taxonomy described in [11] and also in Chap. 1, WallShare is a DUI system represented by a multi-display ecosystem composed by Inch and Perch scale size displays that define a few-few social interaction relationship among users.

From the collaborative perspective, the system provides users with face-to-face collaboration, in the same space, at the same time. The WallShare platform does not provide any way to organize the information in the shared desktop. It is not a big deal when supporting face-to-face meetings, addressing a specific subject for short periods of time (some hours at most); because there are a relatively low number of resources to manage.

Figure 10.1 shows a prototype for a SocialTV [8] setting, which was realized with the WallShare platform. The figure shows people navigating in a SocialTV environment by using their own mobile devices as remote controls. The system allows other groups to see the same content together with this group. For members of crisis teams this means that they do not necessarily have to be located together. For researchers, evaluating the interaction of crisis team members with the WallShare platform, this means that they do not need to be physically present in order to evaluate the usability of the UI.

We called the system which resulted from extending Wallshare "Environment for Secure Cloud Applications by Adaptable Virtualization and Best Practice Consideration" (ESCAVISION). One of the most important functions that ESCAVISION acquires by applying WallShare is that, the system can learn user's preferences in order to assist them. These preferences are represented by user profiles. WallShare asks the user to identify himself and it gets the initial information about the user (e.g. name, age, language, etc.), and our proposed system acquires knowledge about user actions that are worth being recorded to determine their preferences and to model relationships between them. WallShare maintains the status of every device, with which the user makes use of the system, and activates them as per user preference. It generates a sequence of expected user's query and simultaneously activates the devices with preset preference settings.

WallShare per se already offers facilities to distribute the UI. We added additional facilities for an observer UI, which contains exclusive menus for observation purposes. In case that somebody from the "observer" group joins a WallShare session, the DUI turns on observer facilities. Otherwise the UI is restricted to ESCAVISION functions. These functions include selecting applications and cloud services, as well as, defining security properties [9]. The functions mentioned above were integrated in WallShare by means of a sophisticated UI (see Fig. 10.2). Crisis teams can use the UI from different locations, which allows them to work distributed, using their mobile phones as a remote control (see Fig. 10.1). Observers can also be located nearby or at different locations so that regular users cannot see their individual UIs. Additionally, each member of either group can change his/her location without any negative effect on the observation process. Therefore requirements (**R1**) and (**R3**) are fulfilled.

10.4　Related Work

From the origin, WallShare presents a Single display groupware (SDG) [12] that supports face-to-face collaborators working over a single shared display, where all people have their own input device. SDG that supports co-located collaboration has been well researched [13–19]. In general, SDG is intended to enable the participants to share information and actively participate in the discussion. However, WallShare was extended to support geographically distributed teams thus representing a so-called Multi-display groupware (MDG).

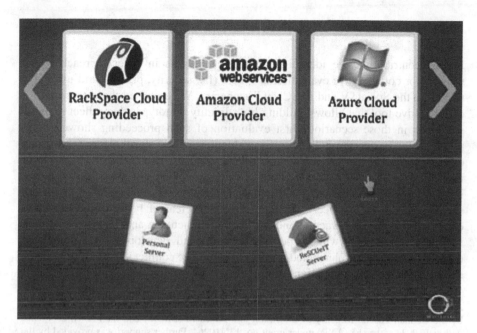

Fig. 10.2 ESCAVISION functions integrated in WallShare

In [6] again, WallShare was used as a DUI to support secure distributed "*Decision Making*". Hence the general eligibility of DUIs for decision-making was shown. However this work did not cover using DUIs as a testing environment to analyze the process of decision-making or to test the usability of UIs.

The approach presented in this contribution is based upon work presented in [8] where a context-aware facility for SocialTV was developed by means of a security meta-model, which was transformed into a concrete UI. This transformation is context-aware and takes subscriptions of users into consideration, in order to decide if certain programs should be shown on a list or not. The approach presented here adapts this idea to decide whether the observer UI should be shown or not.

Cloud deployment was the topic of several works afore. Here we will focus on one approach by Konstantinou et al. [20], which is quite similar to ESCAVISION. The main difference here is that ESCAVISION is more focused on different kinds of users, namely lay and expert users. On the other hand the work of Konstantinou et al. addresses an approach to build applications based upon a repository of pre-built virtual machine images, which then can be deployed in the cloud.

In this contribution we have presented a distributed asynchronous system, which allows remote evaluation of users input; it works in real-time and off-line, processing and showing the results of the interaction. Through the distributed architecture of the system, many deployment scenarios are possible. In both case studies (SocialTV and ReSCUeIT) ESCAVISION allowed for evaluating security and privacy, as well as, their usability by means of WallShare as MDG.

10.5 Conclusions

In this contribution, we identified three requirements in order to reach better support for collaborative evaluation of NFRs (i.e. security, privacy, and usability) related to the SocialTV and ReSCUeIT scenarios. We proposed the extension of a collaborative tool that allows building high-fidelity prototypes that reflect realistic situations in those scenarios. First evaluation of such proceeding showed great potential for easing the collaborative evaluation among stakeholders (end-users, experts, and developers) within agile settings in our case. Especially the extension of the WallShare system to become a multi-display groupware, offers new possibilities, i.e. privacy-preserving evaluation. For instance, end-users could be in another room speaking about their concerns without having the fear of being observed, while experts follow their interaction and the vocal comments in another room. Further, various constellations with respect to experts' and developers' distribution in evaluation could be implemented in order to minimize conflict situations (e.g. when experts criticize implementation etc.).

Acknowledgments This work has been partially supported by the joint project ReSCUeIT, funded by the German Federal Ministry of Education and Research (BMBF) and the French L'Agence nationale de la recherché (ANR) under grant no. 13N10964. Further support was provided by the EU FP7 project digital.me, funded by the EC (FP7/2007–2013) under grant no. 257787 as well as the Spanish CDTI research project CENIT-2008-1019, the CICYT TIN2011-27767-C02-01 project and the regional projects with reference PPII10-0300-4172 and PIIC09-0185-1030.

References

1. Shneiderman, B., Plaisant, C., Cohen, M., & Jacobs, S. (2009). Designing the user interface: Strategies for effective human-computer interaction, 5 edn. In Shneiderman (Ed.).
2. Cranor, L., & Garfinkel, S. (2005). *Security and usability.* Sebastopol: O'Reilly Media.
3. Boyle, M., Neustaedter, C., & Greenberg, S. (2008). Privacy factors in video-based media spaces. In S. Harrision (Ed.), *Media space: 20+ years of mediated life* (pp. 99–124), Springer: London.
4. Palen, L., & Dourish, P. (2003). Unpacking "privacy" for a networked world. *CHI'03: Proceedings of the SIGCHI Conference on Human Factors in Computing Systems* (pp. 129–136). ACM Press, New York.
5. Bourimi, M., & Kesdogan, D. (2013). Experiences by using affine for building collaborative applications for online communities. *Proceedings of the 15th International Conference on Human-Computer Interaction.*
6. Bourimi, M., Barth, T., Kesdogan, D., Abou-Tair, D. D. I., Hermann, F., & Thiel, S. (2012). Using distributed user interfaces in collaborative, secure, and privacy-preserving software environments. *International Journal of Human-Computer Interaction, 28*(11), 748–753.
7. Karatas, F., Barth, T., Kesdogan, D., Fardoun, H., & Villanueva, P. G. (2012). Using distributed user interfaces to evaluate decision making in cloud deployment. *Proceedings of the Distributed User Interfaces 2012 CHI Workshop, Held in Conjunction with 2012 CHI Conference.* ISBN-10:84-695-3318-5.

8. Bourimi, M., Villanueva, P., Daanoun, Y., & Miran, M. (2012). Towards better support for collaborative research by using DUIs with mobile devices: SocialTV navigation design case study. *Proceedings of the Distributed User Interfaces 2012 CHI Workshop, Held in Conjunction with 2012 CHI Conference.* ISBN-10:84-695-3318-5.

9. Karatas, F., Bourimi, M., Barth, T., Kesdogan, D., Gimenez, R., Schwittek, W., & Planaguma, M. (2012). Towards secure and at-runtime tailorable customer-driven public cloud deployment. *IEEE International Conference on Pervasive Computing and Communications Workshops (PERCOM Workshops)*, (pp. 124–130).

10. Villanueva, P. G., Gallud, J. A., & Tesoriero, R. (2010). WallShare: A multi-pointer system for portable devices. *AVI'10: Proceedings of the International Conference on Advanced Visual Interfaces.* ACM Request Permissions.

11. Terrenghi, L., Quigley, A., & Dix, A. (2009). A taxonomy for and analysis of multi-person-display ecosystems. *Personal and Ubiquitous Computing, 13*, 583–598.

12. Zanella, A., & Greenberg, S. (2001). Reducing interference in single display groupware through transparency. *Proceedings of the Seventh Conference on European Conference on Computer Supported Cooperative Work. ECSCW'01* (pp. 339–358). Kluwer Academic, Norwell.

13. DiMicco, J. M., Hollenbach, K. J., Pandolfo, A., & Bender, W. (2007). The impact of increased awareness while face-to-face. Special Issue on Awareness Systems Design. *Human-Computer Interaction, 22*, 1.

14. Tse, E., Histon, J., Scott, S. D., & Greenberg, S. (2004). Avoiding interference: How people use spatial separation and partitioning in SDG workspaces. *Proceedings of CSCW 2004* (pp. 252–261), ACM Press.

15. Morris, M., Paepcke, A., Winograd, T., & Stamberger, J. (2006). TeamTag: Exploring centralized versus replicated controls for co-located tabletop groupware. *Proceedings of CHI 2006* (pp. 1273–1282), ACM Press.

16. Tang, A., Tory, M., Po, B., Neumann, P., & Carpendale, M. S. (2006). Collaborative coupling over tabletop displays. *Proceedings of CHI 2006* (pp. 1181–1190), ACM Press.

17. Stewart, J., Bederson, B., & Druin, A. (1999). Single display groupware: A model for co-present collaboration. *Proceedings of CHI '99* (pp. 286–293), ACM Press.

18. Ichino, J., Takeuchi, K., & Isahara, H. (2006). Face-to-face single display groupware encouraging positive participation. *Adjunct Proceedings of UIST 2006* (pp. 91–92), ACM Press.

19. Morris, M., Huang, A., Paepcke, A., & Winograd, T. (2006). Cooperative gestures: Multi-user gestural interactions for co-located groupware. *Proceedings of CHI 2006* (pp. 1201–1210), ACM Press.

20. Konstantinou, A. V., Eilam, T., Kalantar, M., Totok, A. A., Arnold, W., & Snible, E. (2009). An architecture for virtual solution composition and deployment in infrastructure clouds. *Proceedings of the 3rd International Workshop on Virtualization Technologies in Distributed Computing* (pp. 9–18), ACM Press.

Chapter 11
Distributed and Tangible User Interfaces to Design Interactive Systems for People with Cognitive Disabilities

Elena de la Guía, María D. Lozano, and Víctor M.R. Penichet

Abstract The rapid evolution of technology has changed the way in which we can engage in interactive systems. These days we are witnessing how (MDE) Multi-Device Environments are fast becoming a part of everyday life in today's society. The design of user interfaces which facilitate human computer interaction has become a major challenge. This paper describes the design of an MDE environment based on games aimed at improving cognitive capacities of people with disabilities. For that purpose we have focused on the integration of distributed tangible user interfaces with novel technologies such as NFC, Web, Mobiles, etc.

11.1 Introduction

The spectacular advances in the field of technology in recent years have led to new technological scenarios, among which is Ubiquitous Computing. According to Weiser [1], technology should not be explicitly shown to users, that is, it is not at the sight of the user but offers services to him in an implicit way. Among these scenarios are those denominated MDE (Multi-Devices Environment), which include digital objects and multiple devices working jointly to offer the user a specific service. In these new environments a different kind of interfaces is required, such as DUI (Distributed User Interfaces). According to Niklas Elmqvist in [2], DUI can be defined as a user interface on which its components can be distributed through one or more dimensions. These dimensions are input, output, platform space and time. Interfaces distribution in objects allows us new tangible interaction mechanisms. The term tangible user interfaces TUIs refers to user interfaces which give physical form to digital information, making the parts directly malleable and

E. de la Guía (✉) • M.D. Lozano • V.M.R. Penichet
Computer Systems Department, University of Castilla-La Mancha, Albacete, Spain
e-mail: elenagc84@gmail.com; maria.lozano@uclm.es; victor.penichet@uclm.es

M.D. Lozano et al. (eds.), *Distributed User Interfaces: Usability and Collaboration*,
Human–Computer Interaction Series, DOI 10.1007/978-1-4471-5499-0_11,
© Springer-Verlag London 2013

perceptible [3]. However, the following challenges should be considered: the user needs with respect to interfaces distribution in the space and in different devices in this type of environments represent a major challenge and should be performed in such a way that it is obvious for the user; some other factors, as simplicity or the learning process should also be considered. The design of new systems should not force users to learn new abilities but should perform tasks in a clear way for users, allowing them to focus on their activity by using simple interaction mechanisms.

People with cognitive disabilities usually have learning impairment and present difficulties to perform daily tasks. In order to improve their insertion in society and develop their skills they need to perform cognitive stimulation tasks. Technology is a useful tool which can offer benefits to perform those tasks. More specifically, games are activities which allow users to improve their skills and learning capacities in a fun and entertaining way. This article describes and analyzes the most important points to develop leisure MDE such as, the system architecture, the devices used, the resources available and the design of tangible distributed user interfaces which allow new interaction mechanisms. The prototype developed is called TraInAb (Training Intellectual abilities). It is a game based on collaborative environments and new technologies as: NFC and mobile devices to stimulate people with cognitive disabilities. Finally, we expose of conclusions and future work.

11.2   Related Works

Until recently, our idea about the computation was a computer where we can interact through a screen with a keyboard and a mouse. This situation is dramatically changing. Computation is being inserted into any object and device previously unthinkable. We are witnessing the integration of new environments, also called multi-device environment (MDE). These scenarios consist of multiple, heterogeneous devices distributed in the environment along with screens and other surfaces where the user interfaces can be executed. Some examples of such environments are : *i-Land*, [4] is an interactive system for facilitating collaboration between users through devices such as *Dynawall,* which is an interactive electronic wall; *Coomchairs* are chairs that enable computing and *Interactable*, an interactive table that allows interaction using touchscreen technology. *WallShare* [5] is a collaborative system that allows to distribute the interfaces among different devices such as mobile phones, PDAs, laptops, etc. In addition, it includes an open space to be displayed through a projector on a surface such as a wall. *E-conic* [13] is an application that supports multiple devices sharing information with one another. *WeSpace* [6] is a collaborative work space that integrates a large data wall with a multi user multi touch table, thus allowing groups to explore and visualize data. These new scenarios offer multiple advantages over computers. However, it is necessary to distribute information into different and heterogeneous devices. For this reason, the design of Distributed User Interfaces (DUI) must be taken into account.

Distributed user interfaces can be displayed on different devices: phones, computers, screens, objects, etc. The interfaces that are distributed in objects are called Tangible User Interfaces (TUI) [3]. These are physical objects used as representations and controls for digital information.

There is software focused on improving cognitive abilities, specifically video games. A video game is a software programme created for entertainment and learning purposes in general. It is based on the interaction between one or more persons and an electronic device that executes the game. It is not easy to determine which game is more adequate for cognitive disability players. The barriers that people may find during the activities are complex and varied as described in the works in [7] and [8]. These studies highlight that the key element in the games must be simplicity.

"Serious Games" are games that simulate real situations for people with disabilities, such as shopping in the supermarket. The main objective is to develop the skills that can help them in their daily activities [9]. On the other hand, in Virtual Reality software using helmets, gloves and other simulators, the user may feel more immersed in the game, and it is very engaging and motivating, but the problem is the high cost of devices, and the difficulty in the use of certain devices, In addition a person is required to control the players and devices [10, 11].

The advantages offered by these systems are numerous. They enhance positive attitudes in users while being appealing and encouraging, and providing information quickly. However the system presents the following disadvantages:

- The user needs a minimum knowledge about computer use. Not everybody can use a computer and some devices, like the mouse or the keyboard are not intuitive for people with cognitive disabilities.
- The system requires highly specialized hardware/software which can be expensive (simulators, virtual reality).
- In some games, impaired users may have difficulties finding specific information.

In this paper we propose a system MDE based on collaborative games to stimulate cognitive abilities. The interaction is very simple, is conducted through common objects. The system is developed with Web, NFC and mobiles technologies. In order to develop a usable and intuitive system to people with limitations, we focus has been on the distribution of interfaces in a way effective in the MDE.

11.3 Interactive Triangle

In order to design and develop an MDE scenario we considered an interactive triangle (Fig. 11.1). This is based on the following factors: Users and tasks to be performed, new technologies and devices available in an MDE scenario and tangible distributed user interfaces as an intermediary between users solutions.

Fig. 11.1 Interactive triangle

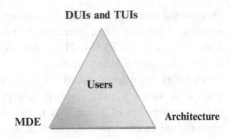

11.3.1   Multi-devices Environment

MDE refers to the devices and the communication among them. In the design we have to keep in mind that all available devices should be easy to use. For example the following devices: Laptop, Smartphone, Kinect, Wii, Tablet, and Projector.

11.3.2   Architecture System

The architecture is client–server mode. It allows any type of device to communicate with others through NFC and Web technologies. Tangible user interfaces incorporate an NFC tag that has written a web address that identifies the object. When the interface approaches the NFC reader (built inside the mobile device) it reads the tag information and executes the corresponding mode on the server.

The server is responsible for interpreting the data sent by the mobile device and simultaneously executing the required action in the other interfaces.

In this type of scenario the server is the main component responsible for communication among devices through an access point. This component is also responsible for the control logic, i.e. contains all services and tools necessary for the rest of devices which make up the system.

11.3.3   DUIs and TUIs

DUIs and TUIs are the links among MDE environments, the architecture and the user together with the task (the latter is an implicit factor that will be considered when designing and developing the system). The combination of this type of interfaces offers the following interaction mechanisms and distribution of information:

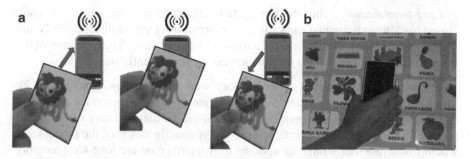

Fig. 11.2 Tangible interaction. (**a**) Using objects. (**b**) Using the mobile device

11.3.4   Interaction Techniques

Two different tangible interaction techniques can be found in this type of MDE environments (see Fig. 11.2):

- *Using physical objects.* To interact with the system the user must simply approach the object or tangible interface to the mobile device which incorporates the NFC reader and will send the information from the tangible interfaces to the MDE system.
- *Using the mobile device*: The interaction is opposite to the previous case, the user must approach the mobile device to the tangible interfaces which are located in a specific place.

11.3.5   Distribution Based on Mind Model

To distribute the user interfaces in the environment we have used cognitive factors as our model. And since the users' mind models work in a distributed way, we have taken advantage of this fact to design systems which are similar to the users' working style in their natural environment.

The mind model is a concept borrowed from psychology to explain the mechanism used by users when interacting with the real world. The users' cognitive system is distributed and is made up of three storage areas: Sensory memory, working or short-term memory and long-term memory.

- *Sensory memory*: It captures and interprets the information through the senses, eyes ears.
- *Short-term memory*: It is a short-term retention store, but more importantly, it is responsible for the information encoding processes as well as for information retrieval, since the information from the LTM (long-term memory) is activated here.

- *Long-term memory*: This memory system can retain information permanently and has almost unlimited capacity. The information is stored unconsciously and comes to consciousness when it is retrieved from that store. The repetition of the task is necessary so that the information can be permanently stored.

In conjunction the three types of memory work in the following manner [12]: The long-term memory is associated with the part of the user interface defined as tangible interface. This part provides physical objects, they are easy to remember and use and allow the user to interact with the system. In this way, the process that would follow the user's mind to store the user interface on the long-term memory is as follows: firstly the user interface is visualized using the sensory memory, then it is displayed again and the image is repeated in the mind by using the short-term memory and finally when the stored image is understood, it is saved in the long-term memory.

11.3.6 Interface Distribution

The interface can be distributed in three different components similar to the user's cognitive models. Each interface will have a different role in the system depending on the information and the task to be displayed.

- *Main Interface*. This interface will use the sensory memory more often It shows the main information to be analyzed by the brain. It is identified as the main working space of applications. The user has to concentrate and pay attention but does not need to store it in memory.
- *Intermediate interface*: It links the main interface and the primary interface. This information is necessary but the user does not need to remember and store it in the memory, for this reason it is associated to short-term memory.
- *Primary or tangible interface*: These interfaces are in continuous use and after repetition the information is saved in the long-term memory, so the user implicitly and unconsciously uses it. They are similar to shortcuts in applications.

There are some considerations to preserve the usability in MDE systems:

1. Visibility of the status of the system. The system must keep users informed on the status of the system. In system which support DUIs the information is distributed in the space, and for this reason we might ask, how can we make the status of the system visible? Which device should show that so the user is not distracted? Most devices can show information in different ways, using voice, text, images, and animation. Any communication means can be used taking into account the device and its screen size.

   - Small screen devices. Images and audio will be used.
   - Large or regular screen devices. Text, image or animation are used. It is advisable that just one device emits the sound so that the user is not distracted.

2. It is necessary to use the user language. That is, using text and tangible interfaces based on common physical objects.
3. Freedom and control for the user. The user must control the system. Navigating in the interfaces must be convenient. More complex tasks must be implicitly performed, making the user believe he is working directly with the objects.
4. Minimizing the user memory load. The user should not memorize the action information; short-term memory load should be reduced. Keeping objects, actions and options visible is better than memorizing. Concerning physical handling, the information from the spatial disposition of the objects allows users to register their position, releasing visual attention to other objects. In this way the requirements of viso-spatial memory are reduced, thus assisting information retrieval and memorization.
5. Offering shortcuts (quick access ways to system functions) using objects, represented with metaphors related to reality.
6. Providing visual and additive guidelines to allow the user know his location and actions. In this way the user can also be guided while using the system. When it is necessary to pay attention to a specific interface, this is communicated using sounds, images or text.

11.3.7 Task Based Distribution

The user interfaces are distributed based on the tasks to be performed. There are three different types:

– *Collaborative tasks*. When the task is collaborative one of its functions is displaying images, text or sound so that all users can see it and be coordinated. The main interface must be distributed in a device larger than 17 in. For example, wall projections which allow perfect visualization of the interface.
– *Individual Tasks*. The distribution of individual tasks will depend on their difficulty. If the task is easy, it is enough to distribute the interfaces into the tangible objects and the mobile device. Otherwise it should be distributed into a larger one.
– *Implicit tasks*. These are performed with no awareness from the user, such as internal communication among devices and the Web service.

11.4 TraInAb System

TraInAb (Training Intellectual Abilities) is an interactive and collaborative game designed to stimulate people with intellectual disabilities.

It integrates a new form of human-computer interaction. The user can interact with the system through everyday objects such as cards, toys, coins . . .

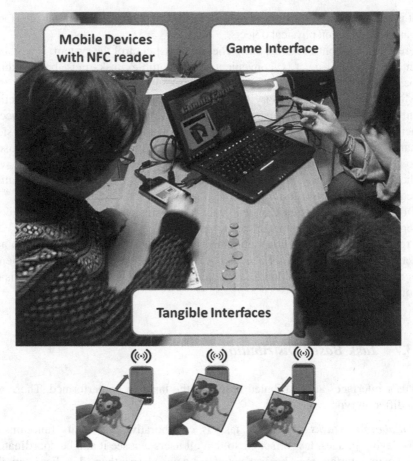

Fig. 11.3 Session of cognitive-impaired users using the TrainInAb system

The collaborative system is based on the distribution of interfaces and device mobility; it offers the possibility to be used individually or by multiple users.

The functionality of the system is as follows. In the main game an interface is projected on the wall. Users with physical interfaces, i.e., the objects that integrate NFC tags, can interact with the main interface; this requires the mobile device that incorporates the NFC reader to interact with the main interface and this is necessary to bring objects to the mobile device. For example, if in the game an object must be associated with another, the user only has to bring the corresponding object closer to the mobile device, and then the system recognizes it and displays the outcome of the game (Fig. 11.3).

11.4.1 Design Through Interactive Triangle

In order to design and develop the system we have considered the three vertices as explained in the previous section.

11.4.2 MDE Settings

Multiple devices are networked in an MDE. In this system we have used the following:

- *Smartphone*: it is used to interact with the system, because of the small screen size it has just been used as an interaction device, the relevance of this device is that it offers a more natural tangible interaction style which is easy to use any size tablet could also be used, being the only requirement to incorporate NFC technology.
- *Laptop:* It is responsible for displaying the main game interface. It has been chosen due to its computing power that allows us to execute quality graphics and multi-modal factor as well as offering sound, text, and graphics.
- *Projector.* This device expands the size of the main interface easily. It also allows multiple players to play at the same time
- *Resources interaction,* i.e. common objects that facilitate interaction with the system.
- *Tangible Menu,* which has been used by therapist, parents, teachers, etc. In this case the interface allows them to control the game remotely.

11.4.3 Interface Distribution

Interface distribution in the environment was as follows:

- *Main Interface.* A projector was chosen as it allows better visualization and improves collaboration among users.
- *Intermediate Interface.* A mobile device is shown. It is only used as a communication device between tangibles interfaces and the main interface. Whenever the user approaches a tangible object, the mobile device emits a sound informing of the correct recognition of the object.
- *Primary or Tangible Interface.* Some tangible interfaces have been designed based on physical objects. They are very easy to use and be assimilated by users. In order to facilitate the use of the system to therapists and parents, tangible menus have been chosen so that they can control the system remotely, change the game, refresh data, exit the game, etc. (Fig. 11.4).

TralnAb (Training Intellectual Abilities)

Fig. 11.4 Menu which allow user to change game, go back, refresh and exit the system

11.4.4 Advantages and Disadvantages

The advantages of this distribution system are: The system can have a private interface (tangible interfaces, each user has their own) so this makes users more confident. Moreover, it provides a shared interface.

– Tangible interaction is more natural for users. They only have to bring the objects closer to the mobile device. In this way we provide flexibility in the space, you can work in the same room and o remotely interact with the system.
– It offers the possibility for multiple users to interact simultaneously, thus facilitating participation.
– In a collaborative environment we can distribute and maintain collaborative interface users' private spaces with their own device. Considering Streng study [14] and the importance of working with individual space, our conclusion is that users are more confident when interacting and working with the system.
– The distribution of user interfaces in the environment allows us to simulate the way people usually work. In order to improve human-computer interaction in multi-device environments that support DUIs it is necessary to know and take into account how mental models and the cognitive system of users work.
– Direct interaction with the objects provides a better understanding of the task. The tangible interfaces emphasize the connection between the body and the cognitive process, thus facilitating thinking through physical actions.

The disadvantage is the scalability of tangible interfaces. These are stationary and designed to engage five users. One of the future works would be to allow users to edit the games and tangible interfaces easily.

11.5   Conclusions and Future Work

A challenge in realizing the benefits of multi-device environments (MDEs) is developing interaction mechanisms which allow use the system easily. In this paper, we described the interactive triangle. It shows the most important points to consider in a MDE system, such as architecture, devices and Distributed and Tangibles User Interfaces as a way attractive and intuitive to interact with the system. In order to test the benefits of this type of systems MDE we developed an application called TraInAb (Training Intellectual Abilities). This is an interactive and collaborative game designed to stimulate people with cognitive disabilities. It integrates a new form of human-computer interaction. The user can interact with the system through everyday objects such as cards, toys, coins. This style of interaction is simple and intuitive; its purpose is to eliminate the technological barrier for people with cognitive disabilities helping them to improve their skills in a funny way.

Acknowledgments This research has been partially supported by the Spanish CICYT research project TIN2011-27767-C02-01 and the regional projects with reference PPII10-0300-4174 and PII2C09-0185-1030. We would like to especially thank Erica Gutierrez and Yolanda Aranda for their collaboration on this project.

References

1. Weiser, M. (1991). The computer for the 21st century. *Scientific American*. ISSN: 1064–4326
2. Elmqvist, N. (2011). Distributed user interfaces: State of the art. *Workshop on Distributed User Interfaces2011 (DUI) at the 29th ACM CHI Conference on Human Factors in Computing Systems 2011*. Vancouver, ISBN:978-84-693-9829-6, 7–12 May 2011.
3. Ishii, H. (2008). Tangible bits: Beyond pixels. *Proceedings of the 2nd International Conference on Tangible and Embedded Interaction*. Bonn, doi:10.1145/1347390.1347392 [8], 18–20 Feb 2008.
4. Streitz, N. A., Geißler, J., Holmer, T., Konomi, S., Müller-Tomfelde, C., Reischl, W., Rexroth, P., Seitz, P., & Steinmetz, R. (1999). i-LAND: An interactive landscape for creativity and innovation. *Proceedings of the SIGCHI Conference on Human Factors in Computing Systems: The CHI is the Limit* (pp. 120–127). Pittsburgh, 15–20 May 1999.
5. González, P., Gallud, J. A., & Tesoriero, R. (2010). WallShare: A collaborative multi-pointer system for portable devices. *PPD10: Workshop on Coupled Display Visual Interfaces*. Rome, 25 May 2010.
6. Wigdor, D., Jian, H., Forlines, C., Borkin, M., & Shen, C. (2009). WeSpace: The design development and deployment of a walk-up and share multi-surface visual collaboration system. *ACM Conference on Human Factors in Computing Systems (CHI)*. ACM Portal, ISBN:978-1-60558-246-7.
7. Dawe, M. (2006). Desperately seeking simplicity: How young adults with cognitive disabilities and their families adopt assistive technologies. *CHI'06: Proceedings of the SIGCHI Conference on Human Factors in Computing Systems* (pp. 1143–1152). ACM, New York.
8. Lewis, C. (2006). Hci and cognitive disabilities. *Interactions, 13*(3), 14–15.
9. Sik Lanyi, C., & Brown, D. J. (2010). Design of serious games for students with intellectual disability. *India HCI 2010/Interaction Design & International Development Conference 2010*. Indian Institute of Technology, Bombay, 20–24 Mar 2010.

10. Standen, P. J., & Brown, D. J. (2005). Virtual reality in the rehabilitation of people with intellectual disabilities, review. *CyberPsychology & Behavior, 8*(3), 272–282.
11. Takacs, B. (2005). Special education & rehabilitation: Teaching and healing with interactive graphics. *Special Issue on Computer Graphics in Education IEEE Computer Graphics and Applications* (pp. 40–48), Sept/Oct 2005.
12. Guía, E., Lozano, M. D., & Penichet, V. M. R. (2012). Interaction and collaboration supported by distributed user interfaces: From GUIs to DUIs. *Proceedings of the 13th International Conference on Interacción Persona-Ordenador*.ACM, Article No. 53. ISBN:978-1-4503-1314-8, doi:10.1145/2379636.2379688Elche. Alicante, 3–5 Oct 2012
13. Nacenta, M. A., Sakurai, S., Yamaguchi, T., Miki, Y., Itoh, Y., Kitamura, Y., Subramanian, S., & Gutwin. C. (2007). E-conic: A perspective-aware interface for multi-display environments. *Proceedings of the ACM Symposium on User Interface Software and Technology* (pp. 279–288).
14. Streng, S., Stegmann, K., Boring, S., Böhm, S., Fischer, F., & Hussmann, H. (2010). Measuring effects of private and shared displays in small-group knowledge sharing processes. *NordiCHI* (pp. 789–792).

Chapter 12
Two Thousand Points of Interaction: Augmenting Paper Notes for a Distributed User Experience

Gunnar Harboe, Gelek Doksam, Lukas Keller, and Elaine M. Huang

Abstract We present two early prototypes of a system that couples an augmented wall of paper notes with multiple handheld devices in order to support the process of affinity diagramming. Our system allows multiple users to work together simultaneously, freely interacting with potentially thousands of physical notes directly, and with a coupled digital representation of the same notes via a smart phone, tablet or PC. We propose the affinity diagramming process as a use-case well suited for distributed user interfaces.

12.1 Introduction

Some activities are not well suited to be performed within the constraints of a traditional computer interface and context of use, and are therefore still accomplished mainly by "manual" (i.e., non-computerized) methods. Distributed user interfaces (DUIs) potentially offer new ways to accomplish these activities. In this paper we examine one such activity, affinity diagramming, and present two prototypes that create a distributed user experience using augmentation of physical objects (up to thousands of paper notes) as well as digital devices.

In the following section we explain the affinity diagramming method as it is carried out today, and discuss why paper-based processes are preferred over desktop computer alternatives. Identifying contributing factors such as support for group interaction and collaboration, tangibility, spatial awareness and interaction richness, we argue that this suggests a potential role for DUI solutions.

G. Harboe (✉) • G. Doksam • L. Keller • E.M. Huang
University of Zurich, Zurich, Switzerland
e-mail: harboe@ifi.uzh.ch; gelek.doksam@uzh.ch; lukas.keller@uzh.ch; huang@ifi.uzh.ch

M.D. Lozano et al. (eds.), *Distributed User Interfaces: Usability and Collaboration*,
Human–Computer Interaction Series, DOI 10.1007/978-1-4471-5499-0_12,
© Springer-Verlag London 2013

We then give an overview of related work, and argue that an approach based on large touch displays presents a barrier to use. Instead we propose a hybrid approach of augmenting the physical diagram and coupling it with additional interactions on standard mobile devices. We describe our design concept for a comprehensive solution, as well as two currently implemented prototypes towards that vision. We conclude by considering the more general applications for this type of distributed user interface.

12.2 Background on Affinity Diagramming

Loose paper notes arranged on a surface are commonly used to support a variety of tasks that involve creativity, design, planning, and organizing or analyzing information. Examples include film storyboards, scrum boards in agile software development, brainstorming, studying for an exam, or planning books on note cards.

One particular process of arranging paper notes on a surface is called *affinity diagramming* (or sometimes the KJ method) [1]. In affinity diagramming, items (e.g. interview quotes, observations) are written down on separate notes, which are placed one by one on a surface (a table, or more often a wall). As the notes are placed, and in moving them around later, they are clustered based on their *affinity*: their similarity or relevance to a shared topic. This leads to the creation of groups, which are then labeled and clustered in a similar way. The process repeats until the highest level has only a few groups. In this way, affinity diagramming is a bottom-up approach to organizing unstructured data into hierarchical categories.

Affinity diagramming is used to several different ends in a number of disciplines, including CSCW and HCI as well as design, business and anthropology, and different variations of the method exist. We will focus on affinity diagramming to support the analysis of qualitative data, or the *affinity analysis* technique, as it is used within user-centered research and design.

12.2.1 Affinity Analysis

Many frequently used data-gathering methods for user-centered design and research (e.g., interviews, probes, participant observations, and focus groups) generate large amounts of unstructured qualitative data. In order to make sense of the information, the teams involved need to immerse themselves in the data, interpret it, and find ways to structure it. Affinity diagramming is one way to do this; other common approaches include coding the data, quantifying it in various ways, and examining and interpreting it in an informal fashion. One of the often-cited advantages of affinity analysis is that it is well suited to collaboration, enabling a team to efficiently generate a shared analysis together (Fig. 12.1) [1–3].

Fig. 12.1 Collaborating on an affinity diagram

A small affinity diagram for data analysis may consist of no more than a hundred notes, and a team of two may complete it in a few hours. At the other end of the scale, large affinity diagrams may contain up to 2000 notes, and teams of six to eight people sometimes work on them for weeks [4].

While a number of special- and general-purpose desktop applications could in principle be used to perform affinity analyses, previous research has found that users of the method still predominantly prefer physical paper notes [4–6] . Among the reasons given for this is that the computer tools do not have the immediacy, portability or flexibility of paper, that they do not adequately support collaboration through simultaneous interaction, that they do not offer the immersion, spatial awareness and tangibility of paper notes on a wall, and they limit the interaction richness to a single mouse cursor, hindering manipulation of multiple notes.

At the same time, the analog process has some definite drawbacks. The whole analysis is embodied in a single physical artifact (the diagram itself), which must typically remain in place throughout the process, and which is easily degraded (e.g., by notes falling down from their assigned places on the wall). As the amount of data increases, the affinity diagram becomes increasingly unwieldy, taking up a great deal of space, making it hard to find particular notes or get an overview of the complete structure, and becoming time-consuming to rearrange.

Once the process is complete, the results of the analysis usually need to be computerized. Also, since the diagram can only represent one way to organize the data, bringing out other dimensions requires the disassembly of the diagram; there is no straightforward way to store multiple versions or maintain a record or history of the process.

12.3   Related Work

In response to the challenges of paper-based affinity diagramming and similar tasks, and mindful of the limitations of desktop applications, several previous authors have built systems based on large interactive displays.

Judge et al. [6] created an all-digital affinity system using a wall-sized multiple-display environment. *The Designers' Environment* [7] is similarly an all-digital system using tablets and an interactive tabletop.

The Designer's Outpost, in contrast, combines an interactive whiteboard with physical paper notes [3] to support design brainstorming, and Geyer et al. [5] use a vertical display and interactive tabletop to capture and create digital copies of physical notes.

While these systems support collaboration, direct manipulation and spatial awareness better than desktop tools, they have their own limitations. The scale of affinity diagram they can comfortably support remains limited, they require sizable investments in dedicated hardware, and to take advantage of any of their features requires an upfront commitment to use them throughout the process, breaking with established practices.

We take a different approach, and while we don't claim our solution is better, we offer another option on the continuum between a wholly analog and a wholly computerized process.

12.4   Our Basis for Design

Instead of imitating the affordances of paper on computer screens, our idea was to support the existing paper-based processes by digitally augmenting the physical notes. In addition to the literature, we were inspired by personal experiences with affinity diagramming, which the first and last author had used in previous projects.

Not only had we faced a number of the problems described above, we had also seen attempts to overcome them. One of these solutions involved having all the notes in a file on the computer, printing them out with an identifying bar code on each, and using a barcode reader to rapidly capture the structure of the diagram upon completion. Another consisted of manually photographing the entire diagram in sections after each session.

Interviews were also conducted with researchers and practitioners who use affinity diagramming and related techniques in their work (nine so far), to gather a wider range of experiences and perspectives, and for the benefit of team members who were less familiar with the affinity method. The first few of these interviews are reported in a previous publication [4].

Based on this information, we came up with the general design concept and decided which use-cases to focus on in the initial prototypes.

12.5 Concept

It was an important design goal to keep the barriers to use as low as possible, so as not to lose the simplicity that is one of the main advantages of paper. Therefore, the design concept relies on off-the-shelf hardware that is likely to already be present in many offices and labs. It is designed to be modular, so that users may include only components they have available and wish to use, and flexible, so that users can move seamlessly between the augmented system and the traditional, plain-paper process. The system will make best-effort attempts to provide as much functionality as possible given the available resources and data.

Figure 12.2 shows an overview of the system in sketch form. The essential element of the system is capturing the content and position of each note on the wall. In one feasible implementation, this is achieved by tagging each note with a unique ID, stored in a 2D barcode (we use QR codes). A camera pointed at the wall can then recognize the barcodes. If the notes are prepared in advance on a computer, the content of each note may simply be looked up in a database using the ID. If the database does not contain the content, the best available picture of the note taken by the camera can be used. OCR or handwriting recognition may potentially be run on this picture in order to convert the content into text form.

Fig. 12.2 Sketch of the augmented paper affinity diagram concept

The system takes advantage of two types of cameras; a stationary, high-resolution camera mounted on a tripod (a) to capture the whole wall, and the handheld cameras in mobile devices such as smart phones (b) and tablets (c). The stationary camera is connected to and controlled by a computer (d), and snaps photos at regular intervals during the affinity sessions, thus providing an incomplete (due to occlusions and barcode recognition failures) record of the locations of each note throughout the process.

If a stationary camera is not used, users of the system may instead photograph the affinity diagram manually, piece by piece. The system should stitch the photos together into one coherent representation, though in this case the temporal resolution of the digital copy will be lower. Data captured from the viewfinder when using the mobile clients to interact with the system can also be used to fill in and update the digital copy.

By moving the physical notes around, users indirectly manipulate the digital model of the diagram; in this way, the paper notes become points of interaction with the system. If they want to interact directly with other aspects of the system (for example to perform a search for a note) or view information that is not visible in the physical diagram, they can use clients running on smart phones, tablets and PCs, as described below.

Finally, a projector (e), connected to a computer running a system client, may be used to overlay output directly on the wall and onto the physical affinity diagram.

12.5.1 Use-Cases

The augmented affinity diagram can support many different tasks. To guide our early design and prototyping efforts, we decided to focus on some simple use-cases: (1) Locating a note on the wall based on its content; (2) Viewing the distribution of a set of notes defined by a certain characteristic; (3) Consulting additional information about a note.

12.6 Implementation

We have created prototypes of the key components of the system, allowing a user to interact through an Android smart phone or tablet client, using the projector to display output and getting input from a stationary camera.

We use a simple client–server architecture, where Android apps on the smart phone and tablet (and what is currently a Java client on the computer connected to the projector and camera) communicate over HTTP with a backend server, which handles any heavy processing and maintains the digital model of the affinity diagram in a database.

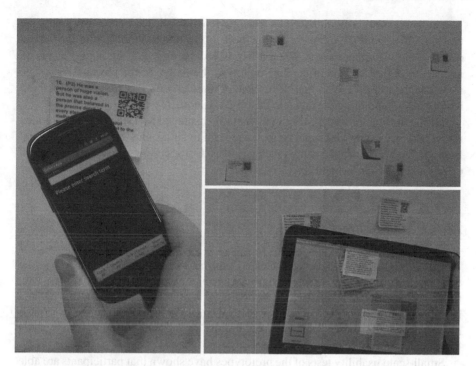

Fig. 12.3 Smart phone and tablet clients; *top right*, notes matching a search being *highlighted in green* by the projector

As part of the initial setup, the projector and stationary camera need to be calibrated to each other, in order to know where to display information that should be overlaid onto the wall. We assume the wall to be a flat surface, and so we simply display 2D barcode patterns at the corners of the projected area. By recognizing these barcodes in a photo from the camera, we can calculate the transformation between the camera view and the projector view and position overlays accordingly. Of course, if the stationary camera is moved, the projector must be recalibrated.

The current smart phone client (Fig. 12.3) offers the ability to search for notes based on their content (use-case 1). A simple search field is used to enter queries, returning matching notes as you type. Notes selected from the results are highlighted on the wall. Through the same interface, a user may also search for categories of notes, such as all notes from a certain interview, and highlight all of them at once (use-case 2).

The current tablet client, meanwhile, is designed for viewing additional information about a note, such as metadata (e.g. the participant profile, or information about the interview or observation session the note came from), photos associated with the note, and direct access to the data in raw form (e.g. the audio or video clip that the note is based on, an unedited transcript, etc.).

The interaction is again based on a magic lens model, where the user holds the tablet up to a note she is interested in more information about, while the screen displays the viewfinder view. When a barcode is recognized, the app overlays an interactive digital version of the note on top of the image of the physical note. The view can then be frozen so that the user may interact with the digital note without having to keep pointing the tablet to the physical note.

The additional information about the note is displayed as a stack of notes hidden under the note itself, which can be expanded out to sit around it and moved around freely in the neighborhood using touch gestures. Color coding is used to distinguish different types of information.

12.6.1 Limitations

These early prototypes have been created both as technology tests and to test the designs. Both aspects still suffer from many rough edges. On the technology side, the biggest challenge is the barcode recognition. While the resolution of the camera is fully able to resolve the barcode pattern, variations in brightness across the image mean that many QR codes fail to be recognized under anything other than optimal lighting conditions.

Small-scale usability tests of the prototypes have shown that participants are able to complete the intended tasks with only minor difficulties, and pointed towards some possible improvements for future iterations. The tests also indicated that the coupling of the physical notes with the digital augmentations is compelling and easily grasped.

Neither the designs nor the implementation are yet sufficiently mature to test in a realistic context, so we cannot say how well they will fit into the affinity diagramming workflow and group interaction.

12.7 Discussion

The augmented affinity diagram offers multi-user interaction distributed over a number of digital devices. However, we believe the more significant aspect of the work for distributed user interfaces is the augmentation and instrumentation of mundane objects, here in the form of paper notes, turning each of them into a point of interaction with the system. This form of ubiquitous computing is a radical break from traditional computer UIs, and here we are barely scratching the surface of its potential and what it means.

Affinity diagrams lend themselves well to this kind of augmentation, as the notes can be tagged to be easy to recognize, and the activity is relatively straightforward to model. However, as different types of sensors become commonplace and computer sensing improves, the same paradigm extends to many other activities that involve distributed interaction with physical objects, such as browsing a book shelf or a shopping aisle, cooking, tidying up and cleaning, and many types of office work. These and others will provide many interesting problems for DUIs to address.

Acknowledgements Thanks to Ioana Ilea and Jonas Minke for their contributions in the early stages of the project.

References

1. Beyer, H., & Holtzblatt, K. (1998). *Contextual design: Defining customer-centered systems.* San Francisco: Morgan Kaufmann.
2. Judge, T. K., Pyla, P. S., McCrickard, D. S., et al. (2008). *Studying group decision making in affinity diagramming.* Technical report published by Virginia Tech: TR-08-16. http://vtechworks.lib.vt.edu/handle/10919/19418.
3. Klemmer, S. R., Newman, M. W., Farrell, R., et al. (2001). The designers' outpost: A tangible interface for collaborative web site. *Proceedings of the 14th Annual ACM Symposium on User Interface Software and Technology* (pp. 1–10).
4. Harboe, G., Minke, J., Ilea, I., & Huang, E. M. (2012). Computer support for collaborative data analysis: Augmenting paper affinity diagrams. *Proceedings of the ACM 2012 Conference on Computer Supported Cooperative Work.*
5. Geyer, F., Pfeil, U., Höchtl, A., et al. (2011). Designing reality-based interfaces for creative group work. *Proceedings of the 8th ACM Conference on Creativity and Cognition* (pp. 165–174). ACM, New York.
6. Judge, T. K., Pyla, P. S., McCrickard, D. S., & Harrison, S. (2008). Using multiple display environments for affinity diagramming. Beyond the laboratory: Supporting authentic collaboration with multiple displays. In *ACM Conference on Computer Supported Cooperative Work (CSCW 2008),* San Diego.
7. Tse, E., Greenberg, S., Shen, C., et al. (2008). Exploring true multi-user multimodal interaction over a digital table. *Proceedings of the 7th ACM Conference on Designing Interactive Systems* (pp. 109–118). ACM, New York.

Chapter 13
Distributed User Interfaces in a Cloud Educational System

Habib M. Fardoun, Antonio Paules Cipres, and Daniyal M. Alghazzwi

Abstract Based on the rapid development of technology-enhanced learning, this paper describes the conceptual process developed for the CSchool educational system, which aims to support administration of the educational process by applying Distributed User Interfaces (DUIs) to cloud services. CSchool encourages students, teachers and parents to use new technologies in the classroom. This implementation happens within the entire educational environment, taking advantage of easy-to-use distributed interfaces to facilitate learning-oriented interaction and collaboration between its users. CSchool is part of the "Escuela 2.0" (School 2.0) project designed to support and engage a large number of Spanish schools; it responds to the need to create and facilitate collaborative learning within the educational process.

13.1 Introduction

In schools, the daily work of teachers and students is focused on educational learning sessions and collaborative work (face-to-face and offline sessions). Beyond the classroom, new technologies are providing more and more tools for users (Moodle, Atutor, Blackboard, Calorina, etc.) [1]. However, these technological systems do not specifically support education, and learning is not a key element in design and development. Instead, these models are based on the advantages teachers and students can find in managing online and distance education [2]. Educational users, like Internet users, are becoming more comfortable using cloud applications

H.M. Fardoun (✉) • D.M. Alghazzwi
IS Department, King Abdulaziz University, Jeddah 21589, Saudi Arabia
e-mail: hfardoun@kau.edu.sa; dghazzawi@kau.edu.sa

A.P. Cipres
Albacete Polytechnic School, Information Systems Department, University of Castilla-La Mancha, Albacete 02071, Spain
e-mail: apcipres@gmail.com

M.D. Lozano et al. (eds.), *Distributed User Interfaces: Usability and Collaboration*, Human–Computer Interaction Series, DOI 10.1007/978-1-4471-5499-0__13, © Springer-Verlag London 2013

as opposed to traditional ones that are installed on their personal computer or device. The potential of these services in the educational world are many: from managing their own platform using Web 2.0 tools to total school management (i.e. Google Apps for Education) or creating their own personal cloud (i.e. SyncBox). But there are still other new technologies such as Distributed User Interfaces (DUIs) that may give more flexibility and interaction between educational users [3]. DUIs help divide tasks between different user interfaces and perform these tasks in more interactive way. A unique user or set of users can do this in a collaborative manner, which is the basis for creating a collaborative educational system. The proposal is to make DUIs available as a service in the cloud so that a teacher can avail of it when needed to perform a task during an educational session.

CSchool (Cloud Services for Schools) is a distributed system that facilitates interaction between diverse members of educational communities (schools, teachers, students, tutors, etc.). CSchool takes advantage of the cloud's services and, at the same time, ensures the quality of the entire educational process [4]. In the last 2 years, the applications TabletNET [5] and eLearniXML [1] were presented as the first step of the educational research. These learning platforms support services and resources such as communication, collaboration, cooperation and evaluation (agenda, discussions, email, exercise, libraries, forum, chat, test, etc.). Such services aim to create a comprehensive educational environment for the classroom and/or distance learning between students, peers and teachers. These tools have been developed to manage such administrative processes for the school's students or a particular class.

This paper presents the merging of the previous applications, TabletNET and eLearniXML, with the cloud so as to take advantage of the current technological and economic benefits offered by cloud computing. With CSchool, schools can identify their core competencies that define the differentiated service provided to those involved [6]. Public providers such as Google Cloud, Amazon Cloud, Azure Cloud, etc. offer some services; others are provided by shared capabilities from other educational systems. Because of this service distribution, unified services provide important leverage. This will both reduce the costs of an educational system as well as facilitate greater user accessibility of the system. If students have use of CSchool free of charge, then the institution alone is responsible for the human resources and financial costs. Students from a state or region now expect such common educational services to be provided via "Cloud Education" (see Fig. 13.1). The model supports interactive applications such as message passing and distributed system interfaces.

This study comprises six sections: The first gives a brief introduction. Section 13.2 reviews cloud computing and its advantages in education. Section 13.3 covers the cloud services supporting these users in an educational environment. Section 13.4 describes the system's services, architecture and charging scheme for the services. Section 13.5 contains sample shots of the application from both teacher and student devices and examples of XML messaging between different clouds and a user interface prototype; it also includes ways the devices can access this distributed system in the cloud. The final section finishes with conclusions and the future scope of this research.

Fig. 13.1 Possible scenarios of the system from different viewpoints: *Classroom* and *break time* in school; *parental control* and *homework time* from home. All connected to the cloud to help studies and enhance the educational process

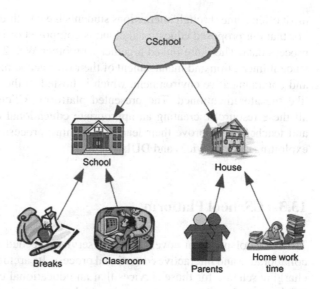

13.2 Cloud Computing

Cloud computing is a new phenomenon linked to Web 2.0 [7]. The term refers to the collection of different services stored on servers that users can access only through the Internet. In other words, the user has access to different software, applications and files stored in different, undefined or virtual places (this is why the term cloud is used) that are permanently available to the user regardless of location [8]. As documents are not physically hosted on computers, they can be accessed anywhere with just an Internet connection. Therefore, working in the cloud means that users don't have to depend on a particular program or even a specific operating system anymore. In addition, the only requirement to start working in the cloud is a device with an Internet connection.

13.2.1 Applying Cloud Computing in Educational Environments

The great advantage of "the cloud" is the sharing of information in a real way. Using a local area network, multiple users can work on the same file, but it can get even more interactive as in the following scenario: a document is shared online by several students; they simultaneously view exercises; they view and edit homework and also organize information shared in a presentation using data from different sources [9]. Cloud-based educational content can, and certainly will, be effective for knowledge transfer, but understanding that information in context, using it to solve problems (i.e. critical thinking) and building on it to create new knowledge are skills that will most often come through interactions students have with educators at an institution. For that our proposed educational cloud is composed of information and academic process data. These are linked together with other Web 2.0 applications to support student interaction and management of their own academic process; a collaborative and communicative environment, which is hosted in the cloud, supports activities like the aforementioned. The presented platform "CSchool" takes advantage of all these resources, creating an appropriate educational environment for students and teachers to improve their learning/teaching process in secondary schools by exploiting cloud services and DUIs.

13.3 CSchool Platform

The CSchool platform covers a set of services needed to promote the proposed collaborative and interactive educational process. Its architecture includes a possible charging scheme for those services that an educational centre wants to offer. The CSchool platform explains the way in which these services are charged and used in the system cloud.

13.3.1 CSchool Services

The cloud is used as a common area for user interaction facilitated by CSchool services using DUIs; this service will be available in the cloud in order to offer concealed support to user devices. Schools being the context of this research, the initial study covered the ways CSchool services are divided, taking into consideration actual school organization in the Spanish educational system [10]. Then, the necessary actors were extracted (as user roles) as well as the scenarios in which the actors act and, finally, the distributed interfaces in which they were screened.

The school schedule used in CSchool is specified following a procedure established by law for management and academic organizations [11]. This is accompanied by qualifications, evaluation, monitoring and communication and is supported by DUIs; with this clarification of the system's function, the most necessary CSchool services can be defined as follows (see Fig. 13.2):

- **Program services:** provide the necessary structure for the teacher to conduct educational activity according to the framework established by national education law [11].
- **Services for teaching units:** provide the structure to develop teaching units and establish the organization of such teaching units to be accessed via DUIs.
- **Services for collaborative learning:** collaborative learning tools or applications that encompass all these needs distributed within multiple user interfaces.

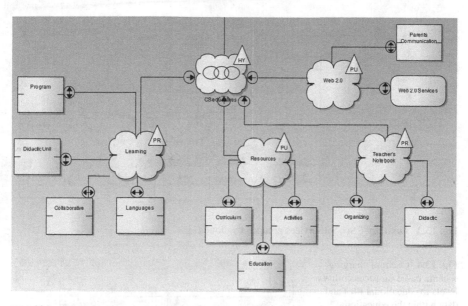

Fig. 13.2 CSchool services grouped by clouds according to the educational process they offer that support the teaching/learning process in a collaborative and communicative way by means of DUI presented by "Web 2.0"

- **Services for learning languages:** distribute the multimedia reinforcement data, audio and video, for students and teachers between several user interfaces.
- **Communication services for parents:** provide one-way communication between schools/teachers and parents/tutors; this communication is developed to support DUI.
- **DUIs:** supported by Web Services 2.0 in the cloud.

These services are grouped in different clouds, which, in turn, are grouped based on the scope of services from the specific educational viewpoint; they can be hosted in public or private clouds, but also include hybrid clouds to support services for external entities. Figure 13.2 shows a SMOF cloud structure [12] following the methodology in which the CSchool services are grouped by IAAS [13], where each cloud offers full service.

13.3.2 CSchool Architecture

Two distinct parts were created for the CSchool conceptual model and system architecture. First, the different pricing types and architecture were defined to cover the different possibilities of cloud services mentioned above; then, the conceptual architecture of the DUI was considered, allowing system users to establish a collaborative and communicative educational process (Fig. 13.3).

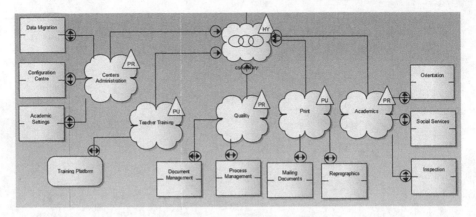

Fig. 13.3 Auxiliary CSchool services grouped by clouds

Fig. 13.4 CSchool charging scheme based on accessibility levels to educational files and data within the educational platform to present them using the DUI service

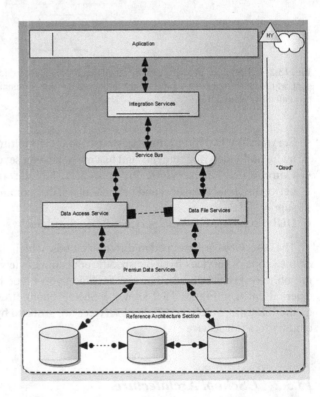

13.3.3 CSchool Charging Scheme

The charging scheme [14] defines the different types of proposed pricing as follows: prepaid charging, constant charging, variable charging, etc. Figure 13.4 presents the CSchool charging scheme based on accessibility levels to files and data.

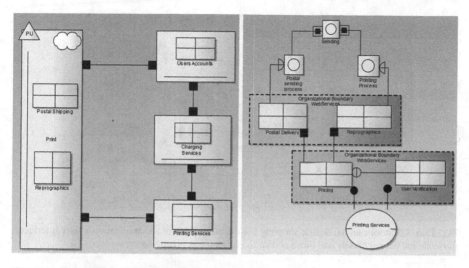

Fig. 13.5 Presentation of CSchool printing scheme and location of web services in different layers and relation of transactions between its different elements

Elements of CSchool charging include:

- System users, constant charging
- File hosting, charging for lodging
- Reprographics, constant charging
- Postal sending,
- Multimedia services, video and audio stream
- Activities and resources for creating lesson plans

To set, store and consult the CSchool charging system results, XML language is used in all the steps carried out in the cloud. The XML charging system allows the possibility of obtaining a detailed scheme grouped by the resource type of charging while also providing all relevant details to the user. In this system, the dependencies between the different cloud services are considered; this is where the layers of basic operation are used as well as any transactions between the different elements. Figure 13.5 contains an example of the chart printing services. It also demonstrates how web services are located in different layers to communicate and send information between them.

13.4   Distributed User Interface Development in CSchool

The CSchool scope and its virtual location in the cloud necessitate the support of DUIs. This is due to the fact that a quality educational system needs to take into account new technologies, mobile devices and multiple uses of these devices

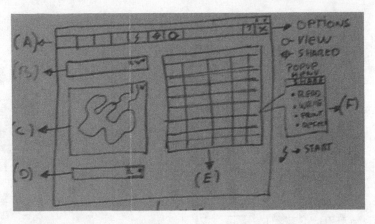

Fig. 13.6 CSchool rational design showing the different parts of the application's user interface: those shared between users and those shown to each user as private sections

simultaneously in the cloud, so that users can interact with the application in a dynamic way. In this scenario, the cloud provides a communication channel for the users to share information in real time. Consequently, specific CSchool services were created to establish user communication and interaction. Thus, the interface's designs as well as distribution methods between several user interfaces are managed in the cloud before being displayed on the user device. These interfaces were developed using Model Driven Architecture (MDA) [15]. Moreover, all educational resources were developed to support DUIs and to share reading (viewing) and writing (editing) properties. The interface application is separated into several sections and divided for distribution between several devices, providing the means for communication and collaboration (see Fig. 13.6).

The rational design described in Fig. 13.6 defines the interface functionality where users can select whether they want to share reading/writing properties of their screen with other users. Section A indicates the menu options for sharing items; "read" and/or "write" properties to be added. By managing A, the user interface will preview these actions on the other interface elements (B, C, D and E). These DUI features designed and developed for CSchool facilitate collaborative work for students and teachers, as well as parents who get involved in the educational process, by interacting in sessions scheduled by the teacher. It also allows for the creation of curriculum materials and pre-configuration of learning activities for inclusion in the teaching units.

13.4.1 CSchool Distributed User Interfaces Architecture

Cloud systems provide DUIs with an environment where they can interact; therefore their architecture provides a workspace where different interfaces can share their information. In order to create the architecture, the interface was divided into parts

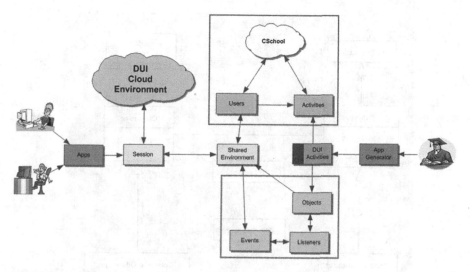

Fig. 13.7 Architecture of the DUI cloud within the CSchool system containing the services offered to the users and its relation with other clouds

or sections to get an interface in which the "sharing" of objects was possible between multiple users not often located in the same place. These objects are part of the services offered by the DUI cloud within the CSchool system. The system sends the parts or sections of the interface to each device and to those who can support the display of the same information in different ways: thus, users can interact and collaborate among themselves to carry out the educational tasks. This architecture works through TCP/IP communication protocols.

This makes the DUI cloud a "Client–server" communication system where clients connect to the server and can interact with the objects; these objects simultaneously inform other clients that they have been modified or are being used (this is achieved with the implementation of events on the server objects "Parts of the shared interfaces"). Figure 13.7 presents the architecture in which the DUI cloud allows users to interact. This architecture is divided into two parts. The items outlined by the red box deal with the management of users and activities; this part allows DUI cloud integration with the different system architectures.

The items outlined by the purple box are the architecture functions. The "Objects" are distributed to the different devices of the users. Once an object is used an "Event" is triggered, and this object reports within its session to the other objects that it is being used; this is done through the "Listener" pattern. We also include the services "Apps" and "Apps Generator", the applications that manage the objects created by the teacher for viewing by the students. Regarding the application for teachers, the "Activities" need to be transformed, which the cloud system can do, to support the DUI environment. This is done through XML files created by an encapsulation of data and allows the generation of activity through events and objects. "DUI Activities", in blue, is responsible for adapting the traffic of information between the system and the DUI cloud.

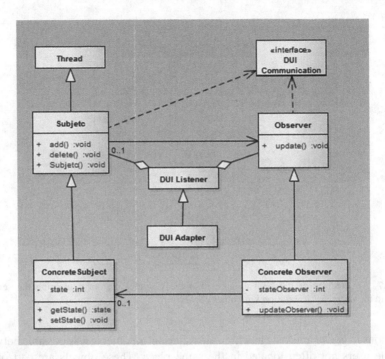

Fig. 13.8 Observer pattern with events to actualize used and modified objects

The system works through a shared environment where users connect to the created sessions that consist of objects containing the activity. The modification and updating feature of the interface follows a similar pattern to that of the observer [16]. This pattern fosters communication between objects and updates the system so that the pattern includes in the objects themselves the elements to facilitate its synchronization with the same communication-oriented methods and to avoid interface blockage. Figure 13.8 presents the observer pattern with the packages of communication that allow the system to operate in a distributed manner. During programming and implementation, communication with the pattern was isolated and adapted to the different interfaces. The "Thread Class" was extended to avoid interface blockages during the receipt of data.

The work session manages the distribution of shared objects for different interfaces and warrants that its use in this session will not result in the loss of information by the user. Its operation is simple; once any user detects a change, the system fires an interface update event, which modifies the contents of the interface in all the devices that share this object. The listener receives the event and updates the interface with the data provided by the event (an event is an object that can store information using methods and properties). In conventional desktop applications, events are triggered when the user action acts on the interface. In this case, however, the user modifies the object in the interface and starts modifying the objects of other users during the session.

13.5   CSchool Presentation

Next, we present screenshots from an activity performed in the classroom and the user interfaces for devices in different scenarios (school, home, etc). In order to start the class, the teacher has to perform several steps; he creates and initializes student sessions so the students' mobile applications will work (see Fig. 13.9).

Once the teacher finishes creating a session, the student can start carrying out the work; the student can usually visualize and complete his schoolwork on his mobile or tablet device (see Fig. 13.10).

Students can carry out their work on their own or, in the future, be remotely monitored by their tutor, who will view the student's screen from a TV or any other smart device that has the application installed.

13.6   Conclusions and Future Work

The CSchool educational system, a work in progress, is presented in this research study in its current state of development. The CSchool initial architecture supports an information system used in schools as part of the Spanish "School 2.0" project. To support CSchool design and development, the actors and scenarios for associated cloud services were defined based on an innovative design idea. The DUI design

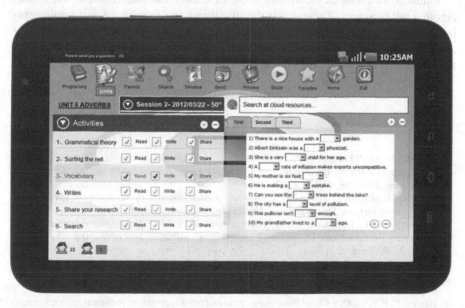

Fig. 13.9 CSchool teacher application shows how the teacher can create a session of activities for a set of students, located in different places, to carry out collaborative work

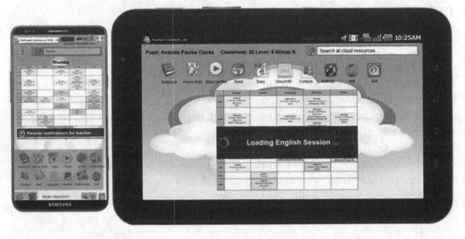

Fig. 13.10 CSchool student application shows how students can carry out collaborative activities from different devices; the same information is presented in different manners

and development improve collaboration within the educational process and act as a roadmap for CSchool analysis, design and implementation. The educational process starts by arranging schedules and lesson plans, developing the teacher's book, etc.; the system needs to operate in external clouds while also serving as the axis of a central system to facilitate the daily work of users.

Future work includes the system implementation and integration to the Cloud. Another future aspect of research is the simplification of the process of implementing distributed interface services in the cloud. It explores the possibility of creating a specific framework for programming these interfaces using a system that allows the interaction of these objects through events in a session created by the teacher.

References

1. Fardoun, H. M., Montero, F., & López Jaquero, V. (2009). eLearniXML: Towards a model-based approach for the development of e-Learning systems considering quality. *Advances in Engineering Software, 40*(12), 1297–1305.
2. Fardoun, H. M. (2011). *eLearniXML: Towards a model-based approach for the development of e-learning systems.* Doctoral thesis, University Castilla-La Mancha.
3. Fardoun, H. M., López, S. R., & Villanueva, P. G. (2011). Improving e-learning using distributed user interfaces. *Distributed User Interfaces workshop proceeding* (pp. 75–85).
4. Biggs, J., & Tang, C. (2011). *Teaching for quality learning at university* (4th ed.). New York/Maidenhead: Society for Research into Higher Education/Open University Press.
5. Paules, A., Fardoun, H. M. & Isarre, J. R. (2009). Gestión De Aula En Centros Educativos. http://tabletnet.linkate.es/. Retrieved 1 June 2013.
6. Barrios, L. F. E. (2009). Cloud computing como una red de servicios. Technical report, Instituto Técnologico de Costa Rica.

7. Grobauer, B., Walloschek, T., & Stocker, E. (2011). Understanding cloud computing vulnerabilities. *IEEE Security and Privacy, 9*(2), 50–57.
8. Gens, F. (2008). Defining "cloud services" and "cloud computing". *IDC Exchange*.http://blogs. idc.com/ie/?p=190. Retrieved 22 Aug 2010.
9. Berrocoso, J. V., Garrido, M., & Sosa, M. J. (2009). *Políticas educativas para la integración de las TIC en Extremadura y sus efectos sobre la innovación didáctica y el proceso enseñanza-aprendizaje: La percepción del profesorado*. Extremadura: University of Extremadura.
10. Arnaiz, P., & Castejón, J. L. (2001). Towards a change in the role of the support teacher in the Spanish education system. *European Journal of Special Needs Education, 16*(2), 99–110.
11. Delgado, M. L. (2011). *Organización de centros educativos: modelos emergergentes*. La Muralla, S.A. ISBN:9788471337979.
12. Methodologies Corporation. (2011). SOMF 2.1. Specifications: Service-oriented discovery and analysis model. http://www.sparxsystems.com/somf. Retrieved 10 June 2013.
13. Djemame, K., Padgett, J., Gourlay, I., & Armstrong, D. (2011). *Brokering of risk-aware service level agreements in grids*. Leeds: University of Leeds.
14. Marti, A. B., & Ibáñez, J. A. (2006). *Modelo de tarificación de servicios para redes móviles de siguiente generación*. Barcelona: Polytechnic University of Catalonia.
15. Wang, H., & Zhang, D. (2003). MDA-based development of e-learning system. http://csdl. computer.org/. Retrieved 10 June 2013.
16. Maier, I., Rompf, T., & Odersky, M. (2010). *Deprecating the observer pattern*. Lausanne: Swiss Federal Institute of Technology.

Printed in the United States
By Bookmasters

Printed in the United States
By Bookmasters